THINKING ABOUT SUICIDE

THINKING ABOUT SUICIDE

contemplating and comprehending the urge to die

DAVID WEBB

PCCS BOOKS
Ross-on-Wye

First published 2010
Reprinted 2010
Reprinted 2011

PCCS BOOKS Ltd.
2 Cropper Row
Alton Road
Ross-on-Wye
Herefordshire
HR9 5LA
UK
Tel +44 (0)1989 763 900
www.pccs-books.co.uk

Thinking About Suicide:
Contemplating and comprehending the urge to die

A CIP catalogue record for this book is available from the British Library

ISBN 978 1 906254 28 5

Cover artwork 'Take your top off' by Helen Martin
Cover designed in the UK by Old Dog Graphics
Typeset in the UK by The Old Dog's Missus
Printed by Bell & Bain, Glasgow, UK

CONTENTS

This book is dedicated to all who struggle with life

FOREWORD

Valerie Walkerdine

I first met David when I went to Victoria University in Melbourne to take part in a workshop on courageous research. I vividly remember sitting in the room hearing about the astonishingly courageous work that David was doing and feeling deeply moved by it.

The book that has grown out of his PhD is a wonderful book. It is quite astounding and depressing that, as David points out, it is so rare in the literature on suicidology to hear the point of view of those with suicidal feelings, that indeed a whole field of research can be constructed which never seems to talk to those it claims to pronounce on. David presents the book in a way that brings together his own narrative set against what is known in the research and medical literature. It is his own search for an understanding and a solution which makes the reading of the research literature so poignant and pointed. And the solution which David finds is not simple but it has a tremendous simplicity, a deeply moving tribute to the embracing of life through being, and its ability to still and to transcend the insistent terror within.

Psychiatry does not get a very good press in this book and justifiably so. It is a terrible indictment of the failure to listen to people such as David and to be able to hear what they are saying. It is not of course, as David makes clear, that there were not many people who tried very hard to help. But somehow they fail to grasp the basic suffering and come up with a solution that allows in rather than stifling the terrible feelings, allowing room for them to be experienced in a different way.

That David finds his solution in a form of spirituality might surprise some. However, what we can take from this is a sense of engaging with the possibility of space, of silence, of holding and

Valerie Walkerdine is Research Professor in the School of Social Sciences, Cardiff University.

containment, in all its simplicity, and thus in finding this, the need no longer to struggle to live but to accept and be able to embrace, life.

The book calls for a broad conversation on suicide. This is so badly needed. It might seem, on first sight, that suicide is to be understood medically. But the book makes it clear that actually medical explanations and interventions can themselves get in the way of understanding the suicidal impulse in a different way. What David presents us with is an attempt to engage with suicidal beingness, the experience of being suicidal, a way of approaching a topic key to the method and theory called phenomenology. The experience of being is both where he begins and where his search ends.

There are many things that make up our experience of course but attempting to understand a phenomenon from the point of view of the experience of the person in question is key. So, in the broad conversation on suicide that this book calls for, attempting to understand the experiences of those who become suicidal is absolutely key.

I work in an area of south Wales which has had a spate of youth male suicides. What is the experience of despair which has led to these? How can we understand and make any successful interventions if we cannot understand the first thing about the experience of this despair? Not by medicalising it but really trying to understand both how it feels and what it means.

David's book is one which demands to be read by those who feel or have felt suicidal and all of those who come into contact with them, either personally or professionally. The book's call for a conversation is long overdue. Let us hope that this wonderful and courageous book can help to start it.

March, 2010

PREFACE

Let's Talk About Suicide

If you've picked this book up because you are currently thinking about suicide for yourself then you are the first and most precious audience that I seek. But this is not a self-help book with a 'cure' for suicidal feelings in seven easy steps. I know of no such easy remedy for the urge to die. Instead, this book invites you to honour and respect your suicidal feelings as real, legitimate and important. I denied my own suicidality for so long; but suppressing these feelings ultimately did not work. So please, honour this agonising struggle and then, with the respect for yourself that this struggle deserves, talk about it.

This conversation begins with your own self-talk. In the first instance, only you know if you are feeling suicidal, so be honest with yourself about it. If you're at all like I was, then there is probably some ambivalence. But if killing yourself begins to surface more and more as the *only* way out of your pain, then I urge you to acknowledge these special feelings. Contemplating suicide is a sacred part of the human story. Ignore the shame and stigma that an ignorant culture imposes on these contemplations, and honour this sacred time if it has arisen in your life. We all ponder our own death at some time, and a great many of us think seriously about taking our lives. Ignore those who say you are suicidal because you are mad, bad or somehow broken. Instead, honour the life story that has brought you to this moment, however sad and painful it might be. Talk to yourself about it, maybe in a journal or just in the privacy of your own mind. And then, when you are ready, share your story and talk about it with someone you feel safe with – preferably sooner rather than later.

Before outlining the major themes of this book and addressing its wider audience, I feel a need to briefly speak a little further directly to my suicidal soulmates. I have said that this is not a self-help book and I am in general very wary of giving advice. Not only am I not a professional counsellor, but I also recall how much good advice I received during my suicidality that was totally out of reach for me. I was advised to 'hang in there, Dave, the pain will pass'. This was true enough – it's just that I found it unbelievable at the time. Then there was all the advice I got for the various problems that I was struggling with, which never quite made sense until I saw that my 'problem' was in fact my life. My problem was that I could not bear being me. Then there's the advice from those mostly well-intentioned people who believed, and sometimes insisted, that what worked for them (with whatever their 'problem' was) would also work for me. This became tiresome. But not as tiresome as those who would be my saviour. I'm even more wary of saviours than I am of those who are keen to offer advice. So I will try to honour your own unique struggle with the urge to die, and resist the very human temptation to dispense advice. This is not what this book is about.

But I have, of course, already given some advice in urging you to please honour and respect your suicidal feelings, and then to talk about them. I must qualify this now with some further advice (and then hopefully shut up with the advice). Although I encourage spending time with and getting closer to your suicidal feelings, I do not encourage *acting* on those feelings. To do so can not only kill you, it can also maim you. It is also *not necessary*. So it is important to distinguish between allowing yourself your suicidal thoughts and acting on these thoughts. Our culture, with its taboos and prejudices against suicide, would typically have us suppress these feelings to try and stop us from 'indulging' them. My advice – my final advice to anyone contemplating suicide – is to *neither suppress nor indulge* any suicidal inclinations. There is a space that can be found between suppressing and indulging these urges. This is a space where we can honestly meet our pain and honour our suicidal feelings without engaging in a furious fight with them. It is a space where these feelings can be felt, spoken of and heard. If we neither suppress nor indulge these feelings, then it can be a safe space where we can begin a conversation about them, first with ourselves, then with others, if need be. It can also be a creative space from which we might find a path away from and beyond our all-consuming urge to die. If you are feeling suicidal then I invite, encourage and, yes, 'advise' you to seek out and spend some time in this space. I have no further specific advice for my suicidal soulmates.

•••

It is almost a cliché in suicide prevention that we need to encourage the suicidal to come forward and speak of their suicidal feelings, as I have already urged my suicidal soulmates to do. Which brings us to some of the other audiences for this book. Who might we talk to?

As a society, we are not very good at talking about suicide. In some ways this is understandable, because two of our greatest fears converge in suicide – our fear of death and our fear of madness. We also find both death and madness ugly, so we tend to look away from them. Confronting these fears, facing the ugliness, and talking about suicide does not come easily. A toxic silence surrounds suicide, a taboo that feeds the ignorance and prejudices that can make talking about our suicidal feelings quite hazardous.

This book calls for a broad community conversation on suicide. This is not just to encourage the suicidal to speak up, but also to help create safe spaces where we can talk of our suicidal feelings. In the current environment of fear, ignorance and prejudice, talking about your suicidal feelings runs the very real risk of finding yourself being judged, locked up and drugged. Suicidal people know this and, like most people, will do their best to prevent it happening to them. We hide our feelings from others, go underground. And the deadly cycle of silence, taboo and prejudice is reinforced. Breaking this cycle requires bringing suicide out of the closet as a major public health issue, which in turn requires the involvement of everyone touched by suicide in our communities – which is all of us.

There is a fundamental flaw at the core of contemporary thinking about suicide; which is the failure to understand suicidality *as it is lived* by those who experience it. This is clear to me not only from my own personal experience of suicidality but also from my research since my recovery. After my recovery, I still felt a need to make sense of my suicidal history, which led me to explore the current thinking about suicide in the public domain, and to my first encounter with the academic and professional discipline of *suicidology*. Suicidology represents our current 'collective wisdom' on suicide and therefore has a crucial role in advising policy makers in suicide prevention strategies and in setting the agenda for the public debate on them. Suicidology also seeks to identify and develop the best 'evidence-based' interventions for suicidal individuals. But the evidence base that suicidology draws on is incomplete and inadequate due to its determined failure to enquire into what suicidality means to those who live it.

This is a serious criticism, which needs to be justified. In this book, I do this first and foremost by sharing some of my story of suicidality. But this is not an autobiography. Each chapter addresses a specific topic related to my journey into and out of suicidality. And in each chapter there are two distinct voices. The first is a *narrative* voice – a first-person voice through which I share some of my personal story. The second voice, following a row of asterisks, is a *commentary* voice. This is a more reflective and considered voice that looks back on my story with the benefit of hindsight. This voice is also informed by my research into suicide – informed, that is, by the contemporary thinking about suicide found in suicidology.

The aim of sharing my first-person voice narratives is not to offer them as some typical suicidal story. I don't believe there is any such thing. Rather, my aim is to assert the legitimacy of this voice, and, through it, the legitimacy of feeling suicidal as a genuine and authentic human experience that is to be honoured and respected rather than suppressed and denied. My wish is that it might also help other suicidal thinkers to find their own voice and to speak of their suicidality. And to know that they are not totally alone, and that survival is possible.

But more than this, I actually need this narrative voice in order to write this book. It is impossible for me to speak solely as the dispassionate, detached, supposedly 'objective' student of suicide. The lived experience of suicidality is chaotic and confused, full of ambiguity and doubt. Anger, fear and other passions are also tangled with the paralysing hopelessness and helplessness. All of this and more must be spoken of. The dispassionate, scholarly voice has its place, but by itself it cannot adequately capture and articulate these essential elements of the suicidal experience as it is lived. For this I need my first-person, narrative voice. This voice cannot be constrained or encumbered by the rigours of academic discourse. With this voice I am free to be angry, confused, contradictory, passionate, maybe even poetic at times. Sure, this can only ever be a partial approximation of the suicidal 'storm in the mind'. But it cannot be left out altogether. To do so would be to hide from the ugly and to neglect much that is important and relevant to a better understanding of suicidality. The narrative voice puts all this 'noise' on the agenda.

The second, commentary voice in each chapter is the voice of my subsequent making sense of my suicidal history, including my recovery. It is the voice of my *current* thinking about suicide, which is very different to my thinking about it when I was actively suicidal. This voice, with the benefit of hindsight and informed by contemporary suicidology, speaks of trying to comprehend rather than contemplate suicide. But this voice does more than just reflect on the personal story found in the narratives. It is also the voice of my critique of the contemporary thinking about suicide in modern suicidology.

The structure of the book falls roughly into two major parts. The first four chapters, which I sometimes call the Bad News part of my story, tell of the suicidal struggle. It starts in Chapter One with a little of my personal history, followed by a commentary on some of the major myths, misunderstandings and misinformation that can be found in contemporary thinking about suicide. The narrative of Chapter Two tries to convey some sense of what it *feels* like to be suicidal, while the commentary explores the personal efforts that we make, but which are frequently overlooked, to deal with these feelings before (and alongside) any formal therapy. Chapter Three tells of escaping my pain through drugs, which was a major distraction from the real issues, as were the drug addiction therapies. Most current thinking about suicide sees it as a mental health issue, but Chapter Four describes and explains how this approach was mostly not very helpful, and, at times, harmful.

The theme that emerges in these Bad News chapters is that suicidality is a *crisis of the self* rather than the consequence of some notional mental illness. This seems obvious, as the self is the 'sui' in suicide, and it is the self which is both the victim and perpetrator of any suicidal act. But this theme is contrary to the current thinking about suicide that sees suicidality largely in terms of mental illness. I don't dispute that mental health issues are relevant to understanding suicidality. It's just that assumptions are already being made when we look at suicidality only through the mental illness lens. First, the mental illness approach pathologises this sacred crisis of the self and sees only a 'broken' individual with symptoms of 'illness' that need to be 'treated'. Although it is life-threatening, suicidality is not an illness in this sense, and this assumption needs to be challenged. Second, viewing suicidality as a crisis of the self is more useful than the mental illness approach because it invites questions and lines of enquiry that can lead to a deeper understanding of suicidality. In particular, it forces us to ask what is the nature of this self that is in crisis? Once again this seems obvious, but our notions of selfhood are barely considered in the current thinking about suicide. Contrary to the assumptions behind the mental illness approach, it is possible to see thinking about suicide as a *healthy* crisis of the self, full of opportunity, despite its risks. Third, viewing suicidality as a crisis of the self corresponds more closely to the lived experience of it, which is where I insist any enquiry must begin. And finally, as we will see, asking these questions about the self that is in crisis has the potential to open up possibilities for a deeper experience of the self, which for some, such as myself, can be a pathway out of suicidality.

The book pauses after the Bad News chapters to explore further this theme of the self in crisis as central to understanding suicidality. This Interlude – a commentary without any preceding narrative – asks the question 'Who Am I?' and looks at contemporary thinking about the self, but not just as it relates to suicide. It shows that modern psychiatry reduces the self to little more than a biochemical robot, which is woefully inadequate for understanding what suicidality means to those who live it. Psychological ideas about the self see the mind as the source and essence of our sense of self, a view that is generally also held in the wider community. This Cartesian notion of the self as 'I think therefore I am' has been challenged on many grounds, and the analysis and discussion in the Interlude conclude that it is perhaps more accurate to say 'I am therefore I think'. That is, we are not who we *think* we are. We are human *beings*, not human thinkings (or human doings) and our enquiry into the self requires that we look into our 'beingness'. Such enquiry can seem somewhat academic at times, and indeed western academic thinking struggles to come to grips with questions about the self and subjectivity. But there is nothing academic about deciding to kill yourself. The Interlude concludes with the observation that at precisely the point where current academic thinking is unable to proceed, spiritual wisdom and spiritual teachings have much to say that is useful. This is the launching pad for the chapters that follow.

This vital 'Who Am I?' question was the key to my recovery. The final three chapters – the Good News chapters – tell of this journey. Chapter Five describes and explains what I now call the *spiritual self-enquiry* that finally set me free of my suicidality after all the 'mental illness' treatments had failed. Chapter Six looks at the obstacles encountered in such an enquiry, essentially our attachment to who we *think* we are, and how to overcome them. Chapter Seven then celebrates the fruits of this enquiry.

In the Good News chapters, the second major theme of the book emerges. This is the theme that spiritual ideas have a valuable contribution to make to our understanding of our sense of self, and therefore to our thinking about suicide. Along with the denial of the legitimacy of the lived experience of suicidal feelings, the denial of spiritual wisdom represents the other major flaw in current thinking about suicide. Although exploring spirit inevitably takes us beyond the rational (and indeed the mental), this does not mean that we cannot talk about it sensibly and rationally.

Spiritual self-enquiry revealed to me a great inner peace and freedom, so that my suicidality (and my drug addiction) simply fell away like a snake shedding a no-longer useful skin. I feel obliged to share this story as my contribution to a better understanding of suicidality, and in the hope that it may be of some help to my suicidal soulmates. But I am not evangelical about this story. The spirituality described here has nothing at all to do with any faith-based religion. Nor is it some New Age 'born again' fundamentalism. There are many paths for cultivating a deeper relationship with spirit (which some might call God), which includes, but is not limited to, the many religious traditions. The path I walked is but one of these paths. Furthermore, I am not proposing spirituality as some universal panacea or 'treatment' for suicidality. Naturally, I feel that it may help others as it helped me. But more than this, spirituality, and particularly spiritual self-enquiry, can help us understand and appreciate more fully the crisis of the self that typically lies at the heart of suicidal feelings. We cannot continue to exclude spiritual wisdom from our thinking about suicide.

1

My Suicidal Career and Other Myths

We must at all times remember,
That the decision to take your own life
Is as vast and complex and mysterious
As life itself.
   Al Alvarez, *The Savage God* [1]

When I opened my eyes all I could see was whiteness all around me. But I knew immediately that this was not heaven and that I had failed. I knew that I was still alive and that something terrible had happened. My body felt stiff and rigid like I'd been lying still for a long time. But I was able to bend my elbows and when I saw my hands I somehow knew exactly what had happened. They were burnt, terribly burnt, though I could feel nothing. Several fingers were shrivelled and bent; the dry, blackened skin looking like it had melted onto the bones. I moaned, and a nurse, more whiteness, appeared in my peripheral vision. She said something like 'Are you OK?' and I said I was going to be sick. I shattered the whiteness by throwing up the most awful black, stinking vomit. A huge spew, all over my white nurse who vainly tried to catch it in a pathetically small kidney dish. Then I passed out.

This was in 1979, in England, and I was twenty-four years old. I still remember it vividly. I didn't know that I had been unconscious for a couple of days. I was not yet aware that the real damage was not to my hands, but to my shoulder and neck. My poor parents were to receive a call from the hospital saying that I had tried to kill myself and that I might lose my arm. I lost both index fingers and a thumb, but they were able to save my arm. I was very lucky.

Except I didn't want to be there at all. I wanted to be dead. One doctor asked me if he was wasting his time working on me - was I going to have another go as soon as he fixed me up? I don't recall my answer. I think I shrugged. Part of my luck in hospital was that I had virtually no infections, the scourge of any recovery from serious burns. I can clearly recall figuring out that it was going to be very hard to finish off the job of killing myself while in intensive care, so the first thing I had to do was get out of there. Preferably as quickly as possible. I still believe that this decision was a factor in my unusually quick and full recovery from the burns.

This suicide attempt was not my first. I had tried a few weeks previously but had only woken up with an awful hangover. My preferred method was to try and overdose using heroin, a drug I had played with a little some years before. So I tried again, this time with what I was sure would be a lethal dose, approximately ten to fifteen times what I would take to just get thoroughly stoned. And it might have worked, except for the fire. I still don't know how it started but those who found me said that it was not a raging fire but more of a slow, smouldering one – just my bed and me. I had planned it carefully, I thought, waiting till the others in the house were asleep. But our early rising neighbours had seen smoke coming from my bedroom window and woke up my housemates. A couple of days later I woke up in the whiteness that was definitely not heaven. Maybe that fire saved my life – I don't know. But I'd learned that heroin is a fickle drug – it will kill you when you don't want it to, and won't kill you when you do want it to.

I returned to Australia in September 1979 with my fastest-ever passage through customs in a wheelchair pushed by my mum. I was still a sick boy and we weren't sure what we were going to do next. Sometimes a suicide attempt is carefully planned, like the one that was interrupted by the fire. At other times, like my next attempt, it is a spur of the moment thing. I think I was still intending to finish off the job but had not yet formulated a plan. Nor did I want to impose on those who were looking after me, especially my parents, so I was patiently waiting, I think, until I could get away from them. But then I woke up one morning and felt so awful that, without thinking, I swallowed all the pills that I had with me. This was a crazy mixture of about two hundred pills, tablets and capsules, which included antibiotics and antihistamines, as well as a lot of sleeping pills and very strong painkillers.

This spontaneous (and stupid) attempt was foiled by that sixth sense mothers can have about their kids. She looked in on me and somehow sensed that I wasn't asleep. An ambulance was called and I got to hospital just in time. I believe I was technically dead for a short while – but they managed to revive me. Again, it was a day or so before I came to, this time with a couple of tubes into my chest connected to one of those beep-beep monitors that I had apparently 'flatlined' for a while. While I was unconscious, my parents had been negotiating with the doctors to try and prevent me being committed to a psych hospital. They were doing pretty well too, I was told later. Until I woke up, that is. There was no one in the room, but there was a pen and paper beside my bed, perhaps left deliberately by the hospital staff. When I realised that I had failed – again! – I wrote on the paper, 'When are you bastards going to let me die?' This, of course, ruined my parents' negotiations, so that when I was well enough to move, I found myself being escorted to Royal Park Psychiatric Hospital as an involuntary patient. Who'd have thought that I'd be making this same trip again, under similar circumstances, some twenty years later?

It was a comical episode for me, this first time for me in the psych lockup. My very own 'One Flew Over the Cuckoo's Nest' experience. Although still drugged and dazed by my overdose and hospitalisation, I was indignant about being locked up, and went on a non-cooperation campaign. I refused any medications except my painkillers and went on a hunger strike. This worked a treat. No, it didn't get me discharged, but after two days of my hunger strike I had the most enormous crap that somehow purged my system and, I have to say, cleared my head. Thinking more clearly now, I was able to figure that the best way out of there was to appear sane. This wasn't too hard. I simply turned on that educated, articulate, middle-class 'charm' I'd learned at the posh private school I'd gone to as a boy. It took a few days, but with the support of my family I was soon discharged.

I felt pretty bad about what I'd done and all the pain and hassles I was causing my family. I moved in with my sister and tried to put suicide out of my mind. I was also booked in for some more surgery on my hand, so I soon found myself back in the familiar territory of a hospital plastics ward. During this time I was encouraged to consider what I might do when I got out. My first decision was that I didn't want to be an 'invalid', that if I was going to live then I still wanted to be responsible for my own livelihood. Next, I looked at my disfigured hands and realised I wasn't going to make much of a living out of them any more, so I thought about going to uni.

Computers were the talk of the day, so I started looking around for computer courses.

I fell out of hospital into the Computer Science department at RMIT (Royal Melbourne Institute of Technology, later to become RMIT University). The first year was a daze, taking regular handfuls of pain-killers and wondering what the hell I was doing here with all the fresh-faced kids straight out of school. But somehow I stuck at it and graduated three years later.

The next fifteen years were a fascinating and rewarding time. The computer software industry at the time was exciting and full of opportunities, and I had some great jobs, including a year in New York. Then in the early 90s I found myself back at RMIT, this time teaching in the same Computer Science department where I'd been a student a decade earlier. I think I'd lost interest in the commercial software world, but, as my great good luck would have it, I found at RMIT that I really loved teaching.

I left RMIT at the end of 1994 under pressure to become a researcher rather than just a teacher, as part of RMIT's transition to becoming a university. It's amusing now to find myself doing a PhD when I didn't want to do one then, but I guess I was never really that interested in computers. So I left - with a sense of freedom and adventure. I was about to turn 40, with no family or other dependants, and with plenty of money in the bank, so I set out to rediscover life after computers. My first step was a trip to India, starting with a 'pilgrimage' to the *kumbha mela*, a huge spiritual gathering on the Ganges, with my old yoga buddy of many years, Susan. I also wanted to revisit the wonderful handloom weaving centres, especially the raw silk ones, that I had known when I lived and worked in India in the mid-70s. And I had a fantasy of maybe writing a novel based on the historical silk road. What fun!

But silly me, my exciting plans were upset by foolishly falling in love not long before I left for India. I found I missed this woman awfully and so returned to Australia after just four weeks. Within a few months we had fallen out of love, and suicidality came rushing back into my life.

After fifteen years, I guess I had come to regard my suicidality of 1979 as some youthful aberration. But even with this history, I didn't initially recognise that it had truly returned. I was brokenhearted and adrift, and also homeless and jobless, though these were both deliberate choices. I should have recognised this pain. And I definitely should have recognised it when I turned to heroin for pain relief. Apart from one brief, silly play with it a few years earlier, I'd not used heroin since the suicide days of '79, and it was not a part of my life or something I pined for. I knew I loved the high of heroin, but I also knew that it came with a very high price, and that life was better without heroin than with it. I had even come to regard it as a 'death drug' - that is, I associated it with suicide. Despite this, I found myself seeking it out, but still didn't recognise it as suicidality returning. I just wanted some temporary relief from this relentless pain of my broken heart.

That first hit after all those years was delicious, and for the few hours that I was stoned I got the pain relief I was looking for. But in the morning the pain was back. And it wasn't too long before I 'needed' another hit of heroin. The roller-coaster ride had begun. A ride that was to take four years, most of my worldly wealth, and very nearly my life.

As I sank deeper into the isolation and loneliness of suicidality - the 'closed world' of the suicidal mind - I started planning my suicide, but still without actually accepting that I was suicidal. Finally, I set a date and collected all the necessary ingredients. I still wanted to do it by overdose, as I basically wanted to just go to sleep and not wake up. But I remembered the fickleness of heroin and so accumulated an assortment of over-the-counter drugs that I would add to the heroin and alcohol. The chosen evening came and I assembled and prepared the ingredients. Along with the mega dose of heroin, I broke open the capsules and crushed the tablets and mixed all these powders together for easy swallowing. I started on the whisky as I settled down to write my suicide notes.

Clearly I must have been ambivalent, or have become ambivalent as I got drunk, because these notes became lengthy and dragged into the night. As the first light of dawn started to appear, I finally realised what I was doing and that, yes, I was suicidal again. It sounds absurd, but right up until then I don't think I had accepted that I was about to die. I hesitated. I tried to muster up all the 'maturity' of my forty-odd years and to think about it sensibly. I decided to go for a walk on St Kilda pier before taking my life. I still felt committed to the decision I'd taken, but allowed myself this moment's hesitation.

St Kilda pier at dawn can be beautiful. I recall that morning as cool with a light breeze, just enough to blow away some of the rather drunken cobwebs in my mind. When I got home and saw all my preparations I knew I had to take them now or do something else. Somewhere in the back of my mind I heard a voice saying something that I never heard back in '79. It was a message that you often hear when people talk about suicide or other emotional trauma. It said simply 'ask for help'. Again I tried to think what was the sensible thing to do. It was very hard. I don't know where this little voice was coming from - it wasn't actually a voice that I heard, it seemed to be some uninvited echo that was almost haunting me. Perhaps it was some lingering 'good sense' within me that I had lost contact with. When I consciously thought about it, it didn't make sense, it was pointless and I didn't want to be alive. But it seemed to be demanding attention.

Almost as some kind of negotiation with this 'voice', I argued with myself that there was no one I could turn to, that there was no-one and nothing that could help me. But I have this most wonderful sister, Barbara. We have always been close and she is an extraordinary person, strong and compassionate, full of love and fun. When I thought of Barbara, I thought that possibly she was someone I could at least say 'Help!' to, even though I didn't believe any help was possible. I phoned my sister.

Barbara knew immediately that my call for help was real. I was not a lad who cried wolf and she knew it. She told me not to do anything, just stay there and that she was on her way round, *now*. I knew that I would not do anything with Barb on her way, but it must have been a terrifyingly slow and tortuous journey across town for her.

My suicidality was now officially out of the closet. By confessing it to my sister I could no longer pretend to myself that I wasn't deeply in the shit. My roller-coaster ride into madness was now a public affair.

Poor Barb, she didn't really know what to do. Who does? But she knew how to just *be* there for me, which is probably the most important thing of all. It is deeply embarrassing to admit to being so totally lost and hopeless, but thankfully I could do this to Barb without too much sense of shame. I don't actually recall what she said at this first encounter with my returned suicidality. She would certainly have been reassuring and probably had some advice and suggestions. But I don't remember. I do recall a period around that time when family and friends regularly kept me company. There was even a period where there was a roster of people to stay with me overnight. There would have been some family discussions, I'm sure, but again I don't recall. Now that others had become involved, I tried to keep myself together. It was tough for everyone.

The first concrete consequence of 'coming out' like this was that people saw that I was using the heroin again and so inevitably their first thoughts were that I had to get off that. This battle was to become a major focus for the next few years as I tried to get off the heroin so that I could then attend to the deeper issues. This focus on my drug addiction was to become a major obstacle to my recovery. It was nearly four years later before I finally realised that I was never going to get off the drugs while I was suicidal. It was four years before I properly dealt with what was at the core of my despair. And when I did, both my suicidality and the heroin addiction fell away and simply disappeared from my life, like a snake shedding a no longer useful skin. But in the meantime, I had a pretty wild roller-coaster to ride.

*   *   *   *   *

The metaphor of a 'suicidal career' in the literature of suicidology is an attempt to highlight the multi-dimensioned complexity of a suicidal history. It can be a useful metaphor if we use it to learn the most important lesson in any study of suicide, which is to be extremely wary of any sweeping generalisations about why someone chooses death rather than life. It also encourages us to think about suicide in a more holistic manner that encompasses the whole person – their body, mind and spirit – within a complex social and historical context.

Although my own story is perhaps an illustration of a suicidal career, I am personally uncomfortable with this metaphor. It defines me too much in terms of my suicidal history, so that it feels like one of those sticky labels that we find so often in mental health, where only the label is seen and the person behind the label becomes invisible. And like some other mental health metaphors, most notably the metaphor of 'mental illness', it can become a dangerous myth if taken too literally.

There are many myths around suicide, and they tend to fall into two categories. The popular myths are those found in the general community and are based largely on fear and ignorance, which, given the taboos around suicide, is hardly surprising, though still hazardous for the suicidal person. The professional myths are those you will likely encounter from the professionals you might turn to for help if you are feeling suicidal, and also suicide prevention academics and bureaucrats. You will find much fear here too, though it is often suppressed by a silly – and distinctly unhelpful – attitude that it is unprofessional to reveal to your clients the fears you feel. And rather than the ignorance that feeds many of the popular myths, it is, typically, prejudice that underpins many of the professional myths.

I'll first mention some of the more pervasive and harmful popular myths; but it is the professional myths that follow them that are of greatest concern. It is the professional myths that lie behind the often inadequate and sometimes harmful interventions we currently find so that, in the end, they are some of the biggest obstacles to more effective suicide prevention.

Popular Myths

It is common in any discussion about suicide to mention some of the popular myths around suicide. Here's a sample from a quick scan of the Internet:

- People who attempt suicide are just selfish or weak.
- People who talk about or attempt suicide are just trying to get attention.
- People who talk about suicide do not kill themselves.
- People who attempt suicide are crazy.
- People who talk about suicide are trying to manipulate others.
- When people become suicidal, they will always be suicidal.
- Most suicides occur without warning.
- You should never ask a suicidal person if they are thinking about suicide because just talking about it will give them the idea.

These are all common but false beliefs about suicide and there are plenty of others that you'll find mentioned in the suicide literature, where you will also find more accurate information to counter these myths. But there are also some others that only rarely, if ever, get mentioned.

It can't really be that hard to kill yourself
A good friend of mine was once tactless enough to say that if he were going to kill himself then he would make sure he got it right first time. In fact it is quite difficult to extinguish the life force within us, especially with modern emergency and medical services. A topic that is much discussed among suicide prevention experts is the lethality of the various methods people use to try to kill themselves. For instance, firearms and throwing yourself under a train are particularly lethal (reliable), hanging and jumping from high places are less so but still very dangerous, and drug overdoses are notoriously unreliable. Despite this, I've met two people who have put a rifle under their chin, pulled the trigger, and survived; and many people have jumped from high places and also survived. One of the hazards of trying to kill yourself is that if you survive it you might also find yourself maimed, with serious and permanent injuries.

The only genuine suicide attempt is a successful one[2]
The myth that it is easy to kill yourself feeds a more serious myth that the only genuine suicide attempt is a successful one, which in turn can be found behind some of the other most popular myths, such as that it's just attention seeking. This myth is especially offensive to those of us who know the seriousness of our intent when we tried, but failed, to kill ourselves. It becomes a particularly insidious myth, though, when we find it among the professional myths discussed below.

Suicide is a cowardly act ... taking the easy way out ...
These myths are a bit like the myth that a suicide attempt is just a cry for help. I admit to being cowardly about pain and not having the courage to jump from a high place, but this is more about the choice of suicide method than about the choice to die. And although some suicides are probably spur-of-the-moment impulses – though this is

also another myth looked at below – I suspect most suicide attempts, such as mine, come after a long and painful struggle. Such a struggle should be respected even if you disapprove of the suicide that it might eventually lead to. Similarly, to suggest that suicide is taking the easy way out is really quite peculiar. It is a very serious decision that I think few people take flippantly. On the contrary, it would be far more helpful if struggling with the decision to live or die was recognised as a heroic struggle.

People are grateful (relieved) when they survive a suicide attempt

Although this is undoubtedly true for some people, it becomes a myth when it is generalised to all cases. Like many others, I was profoundly disappointed when I found myself waking up in hospital, and furious with those who revived me. There is no sense of failure quite like failing at suicide. When this myth is used as a universal generalisation, what it really reveals is a denial in those who utter it, a kind of stubborn refusal to accept the reality that some people choose to die. Such head-in-the-sand attitudes are not helpful.

Suicide is a youth problem

Although this myth is thankfully fading, as the real data become more widely known, it still persists. Its origins can be traced to the alarm that was raised, quite appropriately, about the increase in the rate of suicide among some Australian young people, especially young males in rural areas, during the 1980s and 90s. This was exacerbated by the understandable concern we have when a young life is lost. Indeed, Australia's first suicide prevention program that emerged around this time was specifically focused on youth suicide. But the real data shows that suicide is not particularly a youth issue. And the good news is that, although still of concern, the alarming rate of increase in youth suicides appears to have turned around in recent years.

Suicide is immoral or sinful

This myth is particularly prevalent and particularly unhelpful. Moral or religious – or indeed legal – taboos offer little protection against suicide. While religious fears of sinning may protect some believers (though clearly not all), they are simply irrelevant to many of us these days. There was no moral anguish in my suicidal contemplations, no right or wrong, no good or bad. I was simply looking for a way out of my pain. Negative moral or religious value judgements about suicide are not only a major obstacle to a better understanding of suicide but also an obstacle to helping the suicidal person. I would never seek help from anyone who regarded suicide as sinful or immoral. It's not all that long ago that our legal system in Australia learned this, and suicide was decriminalised so that it could be addressed as a health, not a legal, issue. Unfortunately, the professionals we seek help from are not required to disclose their own moral or religious beliefs about suicide, which can be a very big problem.

Depression is the major cause of suicide
The popular view that depression is the main cause of suicide is the most serious myth about suicide and the biggest obstacle to a better understanding of it. This myth, and also its bastard cousin, the myth that depression is a chemical imbalance in the brain, are not based on any solid scientific evidence but rather on a sustained public relations exercise by the professionals. This is further examined below, but also at greater length in the mental health chapter later on.

Professional Myths
The only genuine suicide attempt is a successful one – revisited
You will find in the suicide literature an argument that suicide prevention should focus on completed, successful suicides rather than unsuccessful suicide attempts. One reason offered for this is the rather pedantic view that, by definition, suicide requires a real death. A related argument is that unsuccessful suicide attempts tell us very little about 'real' – i.e. completed – suicides. There is a common taxonomy among the experts that distinguishes between suicide contemplators, attempters and completers as though they were three very different kinds of behaviours, or indeed three very different kinds of people. Such assertions are actually contradicted by the common knowledge that contemplating suicide is a precursor to any suicidal act, and that, indeed, one of

the strongest indicators of risk of successful suicide is a previous, unsuccessful suicide attempt. Not many people suicide successfully their very first time. This myth is not only the source of its popular equivalent mentioned above, but also of numerous other harmful popular myths. Of more concern, though, is that this myth limits the scope of our enquiry into why people suicide, to a very narrow perspective.

Suicide is an impulsive act

You will also find in the suicide literature the claim that suicide is an impulsive act. The problem with these studies is that they only look at the time between finally taking the decision to kill yourself and then acting on it, which may indeed be quite a short time. But this helps little with our effort to understand why people choose suicide which, as mentioned above, usually follows a long and painful struggle of many months or years. As with the previous myth, this one narrows the scope of our enquiry far too much. We need to investigate the source of suicidal feelings and the often long gestation period between their first arising and our finally, if ever, acting on them.

Suicide is a violent act

Yet another myth found in the expert literature is that suicide, like homicide, is a violent act. Karl Menninger summed up his theory of suicide as *Selbstmord*, or 'self murder', also described as 'murder in the 180th degree'. Although this concept may sometimes be useful for psychoanalysing the motives behind some suicidal urges, it falls into the common trap of being a sweeping generalisation. It also implies a violence that does not correspond with how many people describe their suicidal feelings. While some suicides probably do occur in a fit of frenzied passion, my own experience was that the actual moment of taking that 'killer hit' was really a moment of extraordinary calm. Once the decision has been made and all the preparations taken care of, a sense of relief and even peace can arise when at last the moment comes when all your struggles are finally over. I have heard of others who report similar feelings of calm at this critical moment – indeed this brief moment of peace can sometimes be enough to change your mind. But the myth of the violent, suicidal frenzy persists.

We must teach our kids that suicide is not an option

This myth particularly irritates me. I first heard it one morning on the radio from a well known child psychologist and it made me sit up in bed screaming 'Noooo!' At first glance it seems reasonable enough, one of those seemingly obvious mum and apple pie home-truths. But not to my ears. To me it was not only untrue but dangerous. Suicide *is* a solution. If you kill yourself the pain will stop. Guaranteed! In saying this, I am not in any way advocating suicide, but he should have said that we need to teach our kids that there are *better* options. This may seem like hair-splitting, but consider the consequences. I know that I would never seek help from someone who thinks this, for it would be just another denial of the validity of my feelings. If I am seriously considering suicide then I already know that it is a very real option. And I also know that a person who does not understand this cannot help me. By making this bold assertion, almost stamping his feet in protest, this psychologist automatically makes himself irrelevant to those he seeks to help.

Suicide is a gendered issue

You don't often hear this myth explicitly stated but it sometimes lurks just below the surface of some genuine gender issues in the suicide literature. One occasion when I heard it stated explicitly was by a keynote speaker at a suicide prevention conference, who said that suicide is predominantly a male issue. His argument was based on well-known data that shows a four-to-one ratio between male and female suicides in most countries around the world (China and India being two notable exceptions). This is a huge difference between the sexes, so his argument conceivably had some credibility. But it is contradicted by equally well-known data showing an almost reverse ratio of typically around three female suicide attempts for each male attempt. The first problem with this myth is that it implicitly assumes the related myth that the only genuine suicide attempt is a successful one. But the real gendered issue is not that men are more frequently suicidal than women – on the contrary – but that men tend to use more lethal means when they do decide to kill themselves. Once again, the need is to focus on the full history of suicidal feelings rather than just the act of attempting suicide, whether successfully or not.

Depression is the major cause of suicide – revisited

Suicide is usually regarded as a mental health issue, which in turn associates it with so-called 'mental illness'. These are both assumptions – more myths – that are central to what this book seeks to challenge, so later chapters look at these issues in greater detail. For now, I just wish to highlight that it is a professional myth that is the origin of the pervasive popular myth that depression is the major cause of suicide. Although heavily promoted by the medical profession and drug companies, there is little scientific evidence to support the claim that depression is a genuine medical illness that *causes* suicide. Advocates of this position confuse correlation with causation, because so-called depression, like suicidal feelings, is just another set of symptoms of psychological distress. The great disaster of this myth is that once the professionals assume that depression is the cause rather than just another symptom, they then look no further for whatever the real causes are. And then, typically, they resort to the biological 'solution' of drugs, rather than addressing the psychological, social and spiritual roots of suicidal feelings.

Suicidal behaviour justifies involuntary medical treatment

This myth follows directly from, and relies on, the previous myth, which can be restated as the myth that suicide is primarily a medical issue. Once all these mythical assumptions are made, it then becomes a small step to claim that suicidal people need medical treatment. Another not-so-small step then typically follows, that says we must take this medical treatment regardless of whether we consent to it or not. The argument here is that this enforced medical treatment will save lives, but, once again, there is no real evidence to justify this assertion. If the same rules for testing the efficacy and safety of other medical procedures were applied to forced medical treatment, then the lack of evidence for it would simply not permit it. On the contrary, there is a strong common-sense argument, as well as a recognised human rights argument, that forced medical treatment does more harm than good. I have come to the view that mental health laws such as those we have in Australia actually contribute to the suicide toll rather than reduce it. But no one even dares to investigate whether this might be so.

Conclusions

Although the human rights issues around psychiatric force occupy much of my time and energy these days, they are not the focus or purpose of this book. The purpose of my study of suicide following my recovery was to examine suicidal distress as a crisis of the self rather than the consequence of some notional mental illness. In particular, I wanted to give voice to spiritual needs and values, and spiritual ways of knowing, as relevant and important for our effort to understand suicide better, at least in some cases such as mine. These themes make up the latter part of this book.

But before we can get there, it is necessary to expose and debunk the many common myths and misunderstandings that currently contaminate any discussion of suicide, not only in the general community but amongst many of the professional experts. I have briefly discussed some of these myths here but there are other, even more fundamental, myths that also need to be exposed.

As I studied the academic and professional discipline known as 'suicidology', what first jumped out at me was the almost complete absence of the actual suicidal person. With just a couple of notable exceptions, you never heard directly from the suicidal person in their own words. The first-person voice of those who had actually lived the experience of suicidal feelings was apparently not on the agenda of suicidology. I was bemused and stunned by this, but further study soon showed that this was no accidental oversight but rather the inevitable consequence of ideological assumptions at the very foundations of suicidology.

One of the major references in suicidology is the *Comprehensive Textbook of Suicidology,* edited by three of the best-known people in the field. They define suicidology as 'the *science* of self-destructive behaviors', asserting that 'surely any science worth its salt ought to be true to its name and be as objective as it can, make careful measurements, count something'. Furthermore, '*suicidology has to have some observables*, otherwise it runs the danger of lapsing into mysticism and alchemy'.

This definition of suicidology effectively excludes the first-person knowledge and expertise of those who have lived suicidal feelings, by rejecting them as invalid data. The first-person 'data' are not observable or measurable, and therefore, in the eyes of suicidology, not objective and must be excluded from the discipline.

But a science of suicide based on these assumptions will at best only give a partial and incomplete understanding of suicidal thinking and behaviour. Something vital will always be missing. An understanding of the lived experience of suicidality and what it means *to those who live it* is needed, to complement and complete the efforts of suicidology to understand, explain, predict and prevent suicide.

Suicidology's prejudices against the first-person voice – i.e. first-person data, knowledge and expertise – are neither rational nor scientific. Rather, they need to be seen as an ideological commitment to what some call *scientism*, an obsolete view of science that recognises only one kind of knowledge. This is the same scientism that we find in the medical profession and its hierarchy of what constitutes valid scientific evidence, which may be fine for testing new drugs but is simply inappropriate for understanding the dark invisible interiors of the lived experience.

So the first challenge in my studies was to argue for the legitimacy and importance of the first-person voice of those who have lived suicidal distress, and I wrote some formal academic papers making this argument. But the most important expression of the argument is to give voice to my own experience of suicidal despair through this book. The aim here is not to attempt any generalisations from my individual, personal experience but rather to contribute my story to the meagre body of first-person data currently found in suicidology. A second purpose is to use my story to draw attention to some serious shortcomings in suicidology.

When it came to spiritual needs and values and spiritual ways of knowing, their absence from suicidology was even more complete than the absence of the first-person voice. This can be illustrated by quoting again from the *Comprehensive Textbook of Suicidology,* where, in the preface, the authors acknowledge 'the immense intellectual and spiritual debt that we all owe to our mentors and friends'. Spiritual values and needs, it seems, play a part in the writing of a book, but otherwise receive no other mention in the 600+ pages of what claims to be a comprehensive textbook on the topic of suicide.

To conclude this chapter on the many myths about suicide, the most serious and most harmful myth is the fallacy of scientism at the foundation of suicidology. I have the greatest respect for traditional, empirical, so-called 'objective' science, when it's practised well. The many benefits of this way of knowledge are obvious. But science becomes scientism when it claims objective knowledge as the *only* valid knowledge, and excludes other ways of knowing. This is not good science; it is not even rational. It is ideological, which makes the argument against the prevailing 'collective wisdom' of suicidology not just an intellectual argument but also a political one.

It hurts me personally when I encounter suicidology's blind faith in scientism, because it denies me the validity of my own experience and my own understanding of my suicidal history. This blindness by the experts is especially hurtful in its denial of the spirituality that was the source of my recovery and central to my well-being as I live it today.

But more than any personal hurt for me, the scientism of suicidology perpetuates many of the harmful myths about suicide, and, with them, a shallow and inadequate understanding of what drives some people to choose death rather than life. This is a calamity. Many people continue to take their lives needlessly because of suicidology's ideological commitment to an incomplete and inadequate view of what constitutes valid knowledge. Many people are being deceived into taking drugs and other interventions that often don't help and are sometimes harmful, especially when forced upon them without consent. For some, these abuses from those they seek help from at a time of deep despair can push them over the edge into suicide. But, most of all, people struggling with suicidal distress are not having their struggle respected as it should be and are not receiving the kinds of assistance that would help many of them. The many myths of suicidology are in fact part of the problem of suicide in the world today, rather than part of the solution.

Notes

1. I have searched *The Savage God* several times looking for these words but not found them, so I may be misrepresenting Alvarez here. But I'm just so sure that he said something like this somewhere in his terrific book. I also know that I have 'fine-tuned' these words into the form that appears here. I am unwilling, however, to claim them as my own words as I know that at the very least they are inspired by Alvarez. For me, this short 'quote' not only succinctly captures what we are dealing with here but also reminds me to be humble as we enter into the mystery of suicide.

2. Talking about 'successful' suicides raises one of the many language problems we will encounter in discussing suicide. There are some – including the 'expert' media guidelines for covering suicide stories in the news – who argue that we should refer to 'completed' rather than 'successful' suicides. The reasoning here is to avoid presenting killing yourself as some sort of success, which, at first glance, seems an understandable sentiment. Except that this language denies me my experience of suicidality. I felt I had failed. And I was not happy that I had failed, less still grateful to those who revived me (another mythical expectation that you might encounter). A consequence of this carefully controlled conversation about suicide is that it silences people like me, making us invisible. My perspective, my language, my experience of suicidality are not permitted in this conversation. This might seem like semantic, nit-picking petulance; but I have encountered this censorship of my suicidal language again and again. And it is hurtful. It is also not helpful.

2

What Is It Like to Be Suicidal?

> There is but one truly serious philosophical problem and that is suicide.
>
> The first sentence of *The Myth of Sisyphus* by Albert Camus

I was with my GP once when he wondered aloud what addiction feels like. It was a relevant question for him to ask himself because, as an authorised Methadone doctor, he had many patients who were struggling with addiction. While I pondered how I might describe it to him, he answered it himself. He said that he thought it must be something like holding your breath.

I'm sure you know this feeling but I invite you to do it now. Just hold your breath until you start to really need to take a breath. Then keep holding it a bit longer … then a bit more. You will reach a point where you absolutely must take a breath. Your whole body will be demanding that you take in some air. Don't injure yourself, but, if you can, hold your breath just a little longer. The demand for air will become all-important. It will dominate your consciousness. Everything else in your life will become irrelevant. You are obsessed with the desire for some air. Don't overdo it, but for those of you who have never experienced a serious drug addiction, that all-consuming craving, then this little exercise will give you some idea.

Suicidality is much like this.

My doctor was not enquiring about what it felt like to be addicted to heroin in particular and certainly not about what the heroin high felt like. This craving where everything else becomes secondary seems to be much the same, regardless of your preferred drug. Similarly, this craving seems to be much the same regardless of the circumstances that led to your addiction. Each person's pathway to addiction is probably unique, as each life is unique, though similarities can often be found. Frequently there are some life events on this pathway that led to your taking refuge in drugs (we must include alcohol here as it is just another drug). We can also often identify that some people seem to be particularly vulnerable or susceptible to addiction. The choice of drug (or alcohol) is also quite individual and idiosyncratic. But the craving when you are seriously hooked is much the same.

Suicidality is much like this.

How do you convey a feeling to someone who has never experienced it? How do you describe redness to someone who has been blind since birth? In teaching yoga, I have posed similar questions to the class to make the point that yoga is about doing the practices, not talking about them. I point out that we could study everything there is to know about water and interview at length all the great Olympic swimmers, but we wouldn't really know much at all about swimming until we actually jumped into the pool.

So how do I describe suicidality - *feeling* suicidal - to you? If you have been suicidal then my efforts to describe it here will be shallow compared to what you already know. If you have never been suicidal, then what chance do I have of giving you any real sense of it? And besides, would I really want to be successful in evoking such a feeling in you?

It seems to me that suicidality is a complete mystery for many, maybe most, people. As far as I can tell, my dear sister Barbara, for instance, doesn't have a suicidal cell in her body. I know that she's had hard times in her life, at least as hard as I've had, and I suspect she's had times when she probably wished she were dead. Hasn't everyone? But moments when you wished you were dead are not suicidality. Barbara and I have been very close all our lives and there's probably no one who knows me better than she does. But I suspect I could talk to her about my suicidality till I was blue in the face and this desire to die would still be a mystery to her. I know she has known extreme emotional anguish, and there have been times when we have been able to share this intense feeling with much mutual recognition and great empathy. But not suicidality. As an aside, I must acknowledge that part of my sister's great wisdom is that she never feigns empathy when it is not really present. This is so important because there are few things less 'therapeutic' than someone pretending they know just how you're feeling when it is so obvious that they don't … and we suicidals have very sensitive antennae to such phoney empathy.

I could flip this around and say that I don't understand those for whom suicidality is so totally incomprehensible or out of bounds. Some people might say that I have failed to acquire the necessary social or religious values, but I suspect that dogmatic taboos are actually of little value here. I do not see suicidality as immoral, certainly not a sin. I never have and I doubt if I ever will. It has always seemed a perfectly legitimate option that everyone undeniably has available to them. Of course, I would much prefer it that no one, including myself, felt such despair that they chose to exercise this option, and I would like to do whatever I can to prevent people, including myself, from reaching such a point of despair. But suicide has always made sense to me. It still does.

Suicidality is a legitimate human experience. That is, it is something that some people feel at some times in their life. This is simply undeniable to me. To declare it bad, mad or wrong is to deny a valid human experience. It is valid because it happens and it is real. Sure, some people never have this experience and good luck to them; I could say that I envy these people. But actually I wouldn't say that because I am in fact grateful for my suicidality. It has been such an important part of my life's journey that I could not imagine myself being where I am today without it. And I'm so happy to be me these days.

Which brings me back to the *feeling* of suicidality. For about forty-five years I basically couldn't bear being me. That's not to say that it was forty-five years of constant misery - far from it. The best description I can come up with is that there was a constant sadness in me that I could escape from through various life adventures such as school, travel, lovers or work. But this constant sadness - which I now sometimes call a divine discontent - seemed to be the place I always returned to from these adventures. I don't know why this sadness is within me but it seems to have been there forever. It has always been a part of me. It has always been a part of my sense of who I am; a part, and a significant part, of my sense of self.

Most of the time I travelled with this sadness as a quiet companion. Indeed sometimes I could even pretend that it wasn't there. But it was - always. Sometimes, though, this sadness surfaced in quite powerful ways. It could surface as anger. It could surface as shyness, sometimes an extreme, painful shyness. It could surface as disappointment or feelings of being let down. Most of the time it would surface in response to something that had happened, though sometimes it would seem to rise up for no apparent reason at all. All this seemed pretty ordinary to me. Isn't it the same for everybody? Or so it seemed to me ... and largely still does.

But sometimes – twice so far in this life – this sadness was unleashed in all its force. For me, both these occasions were after a very special love relationship had fallen apart. I have always been quite clear in my own mind, both at the time and still now, that these relationship break-ups were the trigger, not the cause, of my suicidality. As triggers they opened the floodgates of my sadness and I was overwhelmed. Despite my best efforts and all my years of practice at living with and managing this sadness, I was not strong enough when it was unleashed in all its power.

So first of all, for me at least, my suicidality comes from very deep within my being. It may look like an impetuous, spontaneous tantrum, but its source lies deep within me. It might also seem sudden and out of the blue, but it is actually a slow-brewing tide that is only noticed when it overflows the defences. It cannot adequately be described simply in terms of the feelings that are aroused within you when you are actively contemplating suicide. These feelings have a history, they are old, even ancient.

But when these 'actively suicidal' feelings are aroused, the addiction metaphor is not a bad one. There is a craving, a deep, urgent craving. And the holding your breath analogy is not bad either. It is like you're gasping for air, unable to breathe. But it is not air that you are gasping for, it is life. And it is not heroin or alcohol that you crave but peace, some freedom from this anguish. When the suicidality is burning hot inside you, any freedom at all will do. I tried to go to sleep so that I would never wake up – to die by mentally deciding to die. Dammit! I couldn't do it. I begged, even prayed to some Higher Power that I didn't believe in, for my 'madness' to be complete. Lord, let me be a blithering, dribbling idiot in the corner of some loony bin, just let me be free of this pain. Again I was unsuccessful. I tried so many things but none of them worked. Eventually the suicide option became the only option. And, in time, that moment of decision comes.

•••

Some time about half way through my four years of madness I said to a friend that I simply couldn't see a way out of the mess I was in without some change in consciousness that I was unable to imagine. To make my point to this friend I said that it would have to be comparable to the change in consciousness that takes place at puberty. And just as the pre-pubescent child cannot imagine sexual maturity, I was unable to imagine any way that I might ever be comfortable being me again.

I say 'again' because I had enjoyed many times and periods in my life when I felt that life had been very good indeed. I'd had many happy times. I'd had some wonderful adventures and great good fortune. I grew up in a wonderful family with parents who remained happily together for more than fifty years. I'd had a first-class education and some exciting and rewarding years in a career as a professional software developer and university lecturer. I had close and trusted friends who I knew cared for me as I cared for them. And I'd had some truly wonderful intimate love relationships with people who were, and remain, very special to me.

There was pain and disappointment, of course, during all these aspects of living a life. But no more than for many others, as far as I could see. There were also plenty of high times, and more opportunities than most people get, I reckon, for relationships, travel and work. By and large I made the most of these opportunities and reaped some pretty good rewards from them. In summary, you could say that my life had been mostly safe and abundant. So what the hell was the problem with me?

I met people in the drug detox and rehab circuit who longed to return to some earlier time in their lives prior to the ravages of their addictions. But I knew that there was no time in my history that I wanted to return to. I knew that, despite many fond memories, even the best times from my past could not satisfy me now. I knew that even the intimate love relationships that had broken my heart when they collapsed, and that perhaps I still pined for to some extent, could not mend the wound that was bleeding inside me now, even if such an impossible reconciliation became possible. More than that, I knew that it was impossible for any such intimacy to mend or soothe or overcome this black hole of hopelessness inside me, this pain of being me. There was no way out. In my wildest fantasies there was nothing I found that I could hope for.

My thought about some unimaginable change in consciousness was to prove prophetic, but it was way out of reach for me at the time. It was like the encouragement I had received a couple of years earlier, and so many times since, that it will pass, Dave, if you can just hang in there. This good advice is probably true. The problem with it, though, is that I was unable to believe it - unbelievable, inconceivable and impossible.

At the time of these prophetic observations I had already done several laps of the drug rehab circuit, with a few more laps still to come. I'd also spent nearly a year living in a yoga ashram, which was safe and healthy and wonderful. But only if I stayed there. Each time I stepped out of the ashram and visited Melbourne I immediately fell into despair and drug-taking again. After leaving the ashram, I was now living with some friends in beautiful forest country in New South Wales, where, like the ashram, it was safe and healthy and wonderful and I felt that I was maybe getting over my woes.

But I should have known better. During this year with my friends in the forest, I was taking anti-depressant medication and seeing a psychologist each week, and I was not the only one thinking that things were on the improve. You so desperately want to believe that this intolerable life is slowly, bit by bit, becoming tolerable again. You want to believe that being me does not have to be so bloody awful. That somehow I will learn how to live in this skin. You want to believe this so much because you want it to come true. You also want to believe it because the people around you want to believe it too. You really really want to believe it, so sometimes you actually do.

But with hindsight I can say that even at the time, in my heart of hearts, I knew that it wasn't true. During this year in this beautiful place, living a simple, healthy life with wonderful friends, I was largely a recluse. I enjoyed the company with these two dear people, but beyond that I socialised little. I did not want to participate in the world, and had fantasies about becoming some sort of a monk, perhaps a yoga swami (although I had already ruled this out many years before). I would talk of being in 'retreat' but I was really hiding from the world. I did not want to get too close or be too close to anyone. It was not so much a retreat as an escape.

But I could not escape from myself. Not all the time. I could put on a pretence of being 'sane' as I worked not to disengage altogether from the world around me. I could present a personality to this outer world that most people could tolerate as acceptable, but it was an effort, and I felt it was false and unreal. I could talk to the psychologist, as well as friends, about my feelings and the 'progress' I was making. I was intelligent, honest and articulate about my feelings and circumstances, and tried hard - oh so hard - to be open to the possibility that I was actually getting 'better'. I tried to accept that this bottomless bucket of shit that I lived in within myself was just the human condition and that I had to learn to accept that. I tried so hard to believe this. If I could just let go of my unrealistic expectations of life being anything other than a bucket of shit, then I might actually find some useful meaning and purpose to being me. I didn't have a clue. Deep down, in the privacy of solitude, there was no meaning to it at all, and, more than that, no meaning was possible. But I tried hard to believe otherwise, and at times I managed to convince myself of this. I believed it because I wanted and needed to and because those around me wanted and needed to believe it too. But it wasn't true.

In many ways it was a very good year for me, and I treasure the memory of it, but it was bloody hard work. And it didn't work. I left there at the start of 1998 thinking that I was OK, or close to it. I was soon back on the heroin, and the worst was yet to come.

*   *   *   *   *

Hopelessness and helplessness are the two words most frequently associated with suicide. We hear this first of all from suicidal people themselves, but there is also general agreement among suicide prevention experts about the significance of these two emotions. Unfortunately these experts only rarely delve deeper to explore the source of these feelings and what they mean to those who live them.

Hopelessness to me is the 'black hole' of despair, or sometimes a profound feeling of utter emptiness inside. And helplessness is the belief that this empty, black hole is forever, that it could never be otherwise. An image I have of this is of being at the bottom of a very deep well, a black hole of meaningless emptiness. This is the hopelessness. And the exit from this deep, dark well is so far up that it can't be seen; and the walls are so dark and smooth and greasy that it's impossible to get any hold on them at all. This is the helplessness.

I suspect that both these ingredients are probably necessary for suicidality to arise, but it is hopelessness that is the critical one: it is hopelessness that says life is not worth living; it is hopelessness that is the source of the agony and despair. And underneath the hopelessness is the feeling that life is meaningless – hopelessness and meaninglessness go hand in hand for me. And then the helplessness says that this agony will last forever, that nothing but meaningless hopelessness is possible.

Hopelessness and helplessness can only be fully known through the living of them – through their lived experience or, in short, though our *feelings*. Subjective, lived feelings are what lead us to suicidal despair. It is these feelings, so intimately personal, private and often secret, which lead us to choose death rather than life. Suicide occurs because of an invisible *decision*, a very deliberate, cognitive, psychological decision. These feelings are critical if we wish to understand suicide, for the simple reason that they are what matters most for those who live them. Feelings matter. We cannot investigate suicide, whether it's our own personal struggle with suicidal feelings or as a professional suicide prevention expert, if we ignore these invisible, subjective, lived feelings. Regrettably, suicide prevention experts tend to pay scant attention to them.

When I investigated my suicidal feelings, so many possibilities arose. Some were pretty unpleasant to contemplate, such as that I was just being a spoilt brat having a middle-aged tantrum because I wasn't getting what I wanted. Some of the therapists I later saw clearly thought this too. But calling suicidal despair a tantrum does not explain anything and is not very helpful. Another possibility was a typical mid-life crisis, which is perhaps sanitised language for a middle-aged tantrum. I think it was around this time that I read *Manhood* by Steve Biddulph, and much of what he said about the male mid-life crisis made sense to me. But it still didn't sufficiently explain why I sometimes felt so rotten or why I sometimes beat myself up because of those feelings. I can now see that a recurrent theme throughout my life has been these two questions – why do I sometimes feel *such* despair, and why am I then sometimes tempted by suicide? The two questions still remain with me today, although I now at least have some sense (but only some) of the answers to them. The good news is that a complete answer to these questions is not necessary in order to find peace with yourself. This is very good news.

Notice again that the key feature of these questions is their subjectivity. That is, we ask ourselves questions that have personal meaning and relevance for us. And, most importantly, any answers we might come up with have to make sense in ways that satisfy us personally – they have to *feel* right, not just be a persuasive intellectual argument. There is a kind of knowing that we all recognise as that 'gut feel' kind where we just *know* it is right because it *feels* right. We can be misled by these feelings, that's for sure, so we need to be cautious. Sometimes what initially seems true turns out to be only a partial truth or a stepping stone as we explore it more deeply. Sometimes it turns out that our gut feel is just plain wrong. We need to be mindful of these pitfalls, especially when we are distressed, confused, chaotic and vulnerable. Good friends or a skilled counsellor can help us with this, but this sense of 'knowingness' that arises from deep within will ultimately be necessary to satisfy us fully, or these questions will linger and perhaps haunt us. Again, these invisible, internal, subjective feelings and thoughts – directly experienced subjectively and then reflected upon through personal introspection that is also subjectively felt – are important for the simple reason that they are what matter most to us.

My personal introspections at the time came up with all sorts of possible explanations for why I felt so rotten, though none of them was ever quite adequate, either by itself or in combination. As this is not an autobiography I'll only briefly mention some of the key thoughts that surfaced through these introspections. These thoughts usually come up by trawling through your personal history, looking for significant events or circumstances that might reveal the sources of your despair. Many 'depth psychology' techniques are based on a similar enquiry into your past, and some try to delve a little deeper into your subconscious via dreams, hypnosis or other methods. Indeed, once you get on the therapy merry-go-round, you get quite tired of being asked about your family history (especially your Mum). This 'guided introspection' by a skilled therapist can be a useful aid to your own all-important making sense of your feelings, but I would emphasise again that it is invisible, internal, subjective feelings that we are working with here.

Several things stand out immediately for me when I look at my personal history and personality. First, I have always felt shy, and, second, I have always felt something of a misfit. Whether one is the cause of the other has always been impossible to tell. I've just never quite felt that I've ever fitted in anywhere. To some extent this remains true today, but is now thankfully of much less concern to me than it used to be. I was also clever, always being close to the top of the class, and good at sport. Perhaps because of these talents, I often felt somewhat burdened by expectations that I could not possibly live up to. I was also always a thoughtful, sensitive kid, naturally introspective and reflective in the privacy of my own time and my own mind. But to some this was apparently contradicted by the vigour with which I enjoyed my sport and also by the fact that I was not infrequently in trouble at school as a 'naughty boy'. I think I was often pretty bored and used to 'play up' to amuse myself and perhaps also as a clumsy attempt to make friends and fit in. With hindsight, I can see that there had always been a mismatch between my inner, private world and the apparent exuberance of my sporting activities and naughty entertainments.

The misfit feeling of being something of a square peg in a round hole also means that attempts to squeeze me into a shape that was completely wrong for me have always hurt and often made me angry. I still feel this today, though I have learned many 'tricks' over the years to live with it more comfortably now than I did in the past. And with the anger has come resistance. Whether this is arrogance, pride, or self-indulgent vanity, as some might suggest, is not really relevant, although I have agonised over these and other uncomfortable possibilities many times over the years. My rebellion against pressure to conform to something that I don't believe in – to be or become someone I don't want to be – has been a constant battleground. I'm sure that many times I have rebelled needlessly and probably inappropriately. But I am equally sure that it has often been perfectly legitimate and appropriate, such as when I refused to allow a teacher at school to hit me. This conflict with the world around me, along with the anger that often goes with it, has arisen again and again for me. I've often felt that I've been asked to accept the unacceptable, and I then flounder, and sometimes flail about, as I try to reconcile this conflict. And I've often found myself wondering whether it is me or the world that is mad.

Closely related to this 'misfit in the world' feeling is another conflict. This is the mismatch between the 'in-here' feeling of being me and the 'out-there' perception that others seemed to have of who I was – as best I could judge it, that is. For example, I've said that I was shy but was often seen as extrovert, boisterous, even aggressive and perhaps a little 'wild'. In contrast, I have always thought of myself as thoughtful, gentle and sensitive. I guess I'm saying that these were the qualities that I valued most about myself. I've wondered sometimes whether I was just living up to expectations around me, but I've never got very far with trying to see myself through other people's eyes. What I have felt strongly, from my earliest childhood to the present, and most strongly during my suicidal periods, is the feeling that I was invisible. Not physically invisible, but that the 'real me' that I sensed so clearly from the inside and was so important to me, seemed to be largely invisible to those around me. I think I just couldn't figure it out. And didn't have a clue what to do about it. This frustrating tension, and at times conflict, between the 'in-here' and 'out-there' – between subjective and objective realities – has always been there for me with no way to reconcile it or live happily with it. Until recently, that is.

The final personal characteristic that I believe contributed to my suicidal feelings was an intense curiosity, a quality that I do not think is at all peculiar to me among my suicidal soulmates. This intense curiosity could be described as the urge of the naturally creative intelligence that we see in kids. I now see this in more adult terms, particularly in regard to suicide, as a great yearning. This yearning to enquire, to know, to understand, to search for genuinely satisfactory and meaningful answers to my questions, has also been with me always. With this burning curiosity and yearning there is also a passion. If I was truly interested in something then second best answers were never good enough for me. There was always an urgent yearning, wanting to make sense of this life I was trying to live and the world in which I was trying to live it. I was passionate, inquisitive, clever, sensitive, thoughtful and adventurous. But also a confused misfit, angry, shy and pretty inept socially.

These are the personal qualities that I recognise in myself and which resonate for me as elements of my suicidal hopelessness. These are the characteristics that have the most salience for me in my efforts to understand the intimately personal feelings of meaning and purpose that my hopelessness was struggling with. These issues and questions that had been a lifelong struggle, a quest even, were the issues and questions that now overflowed into my consciousness when I was struck by the grief of a great love lost. Why was I such a misfit? Why did I find being me so damned difficult? With all the talent and good fortune with which I had been blessed, how come I couldn't appreciate this and just make the most of it? Sad and angry, my outer world had collapsed and held no interest for me at all. Sad and angry, my inner world was bewildered and overwhelmed. I didn't have a clue what to do.

In 1995 (unlike 1979) this wasn't altogether true, as I did call out for help. But what I found then, despite the very best intentions of (most of) those around me, was that I felt only more invisible, adding to my pain and my suicidality. My soul was dying and nobody could even see it, far less do anything about it. The inevitable conclusion was that it had to be true – I was just a misfit, unable to live either in this world or this body. Hopeless, totally and utterly bloody hopeless. And it could never be otherwise. There was only one option left.

This description of my own search for explanations of my suicidality is far from complete. I have chosen to highlight these fragments of my personal introspections for several reasons. First of all, some of this introspective self-enquiry invariably occurs *before* you get to the point where you reach out for professional help. This needs to be acknowledged and respected more than it currently is; by ourselves as we struggle with these feelings, but also by the professionals when we do eventually meet them. Many people who contemplate suicide do manage to resolve their pain and despair by themselves without ever seeking professional help, though perhaps with the help of family and friends. We all usually prefer to deal with these difficulties ourselves, and most of the time we do this pretty well. This is not to discourage anyone from seeking help. Knowing the right time to seek help is important, and sooner is probably better than later. But if we are to prevent these feelings from escalating into potentially dangerous behaviour then it is important to acknowledge them honestly and give them the legitimacy they deserve. To honour them as real, genuine and significant feelings, rather than repress, suppress or hide from them as some shameful character flaw, or pretend they are some embarrassing illness. There is much we can do to heal our wounds ourselves – we do it all the time – but this requires that we respect our suffering. This also applies to any professional help that we might consider. If a therapist does not respect your 'inner voice' – which unfortunately occurs far too often – then just leave quickly.

A second reason for this choice of fragments from my story is to highlight the subjective nature of what we are dealing with here. This seems altogether too obvious, but it just makes it all the more surprising that the subjective, lived experience of suicidal feelings is so regularly ignored or dismissed in the expert discussion on suicide.

The academic and professional discipline of suicidology strives hard to be an objective science, but in doing so renders itself virtually blind to what are in fact the most 'substantial' and important issues being faced by the suicidal person. To me, as someone who has lived with and recovered from persistent suicidal feelings, when I look at the academic discipline of suicidology, it feels as if the expert 'suicidologists' are looking at us through the wrong end of their telescope. Their remote, long-distance (objective, empirical) view of suicide transforms the subjective reality and the *meaning* of the suicidal crisis of the self – that is, the actual suicidal person – into almost invisible pinpricks in the far distance.

The final reason for highlighting these aspects from my own story is that, after much careful reflection in the light of my recovery, I can now say with certainty that these were the issues central to both my suicidality and my recovery. When I look for those personality traits that were most significant to my suicidality, the ones that resonate most for me are my thoughtfulness, my sensitivity and my 'creative intelligence'. I also see my passionate curiosity and yearning, mixed with my willingness, indeed my need, to explore the boundaries and to be adventurous. This is not the whole story, but I do see them as significant factors contributing to my becoming suicidal under certain circumstances.

These personal characteristics, which would usually be regarded as not only perfectly 'normal' but even as quite worthy, are largely unexamined by suicidology, with its emphasis on illness and pathology. As I now seek out other suicide stories, what I hear again and again is of a suicidal personality that is not so dissimilar to mine. Time and again in these suicidal stories I hear of gentleness and sensitivity, of a sharp, keen intelligence, and a passionate yearning. What is alarming is how little we hear of this in suicidology. With a few notable exceptions, suicidology has shown little interest in these very human personality traits in its search for 'risk factors'. Suicidology today is preoccupied with medical, 'mental illness' models of suicidality that inevitably pathologise the individual in quite negative ways, with often harmful consequences.

I have tried in this chapter, in both the narrative and the commentary, to give some sense of what it is actually like to live and experience suicidal feelings. In academic terms this is called the 'phenomenology' of suicidality, which can be stated more simply as the question, 'What is it like to be suicidal?' As I have said, I do not attempt to make any generalisations from my own, individual experience. But my reflections on this personal story since my recovery, and also my research into suicidology, tell me that insufficient attention has been given to this fundamental question in our efforts to understand and respond to suicide. The subjective, lived experience of suicidal feelings is currently barely on the radar of mainstream suicidology. We therefore find that what is often most significant for the actual suicidal person is overlooked, ignored or (even worse) deliberately denied and dismissed as either irrelevant or (even worse still) as the symptoms of some supposed illness. Suicide as a crisis of personal meaning – a crisis of the self – is not a topic of any major discussion by the experts. I wish to challenge this situation because I don't see how we can begin to understand suicide without giving serious consideration to what suicidal feelings mean to those who live them. Similarly, any efforts to intervene or 'treat' suicidal feelings will inevitably be flawed without this first-person knowledge.

I am occasionally asked these days what I would say to someone who was actively suicidal. My answer is always the same. First and foremost, I urge my suicidal soulmates to respect and honour their own feelings as meaningful, significant and perfectly legitimate human feelings. I am not a therapist or a counsellor so I never pretend to be one and always explicitly state this – interestingly, this has so far always been met with a sigh of relief. But I try to do my best to truly honour their suicidal story as a noble struggle of the self, with the self. Such encounters can be quite frightening, and this too needs to be honoured and respected – my own fears as well as the fears that are invariably being felt by the suicidal person at these times. And how can I best honour this person and their noble struggle? For me, I say that I can listen to their story, share a little of my own, and, if they are interested, tell them a bit about my current research into suicide and suicidology. So far, sharing our stories appears to have been of rather more interest than my academic research ... the sad plight of the poor misunderstood and maligned academic ...

This brings us back to one of the central themes of this book – the theme of story-telling. To listen to someone else's story without judgement and resisting the urge to offer advice is the first and perhaps most important gift you can give in order to honour their story, to honour their pain and struggle, to honour *them*. Sharing some of your own story also honours such an encounter, but not if it's presented as advice – that dreaded 'what worked for me will also work for you' kind of advice. Few things are as comforting and reassuring – and potentially healing – as recognising your own story, or parts of it, in someone else's story. You can feel not quite so alone in what is an awfully lonely space. You can feel that perhaps survival is a possibility. You might also find that you can say things and talk about things that it has been impossible to talk about with anyone else. This might even include some shocking black humour that would horrify anyone eavesdropping on the conversation. And to be able to laugh with another suicidal soulmate about suicidal thoughts and feelings can be a wonderful and truly liberating joy.

This story-telling theme is central to the topic of this chapter. Story-telling is the key to any enquiry into the question that this chapter asks: 'What is it like to be suicidal?' Story-telling allows, respects and reveals the full depth and richness of subjective, lived experience like no other form of enquiry. Stories, of all kinds – whether told in conversation, in writing, or through art, music, dance and theatre – are how we explore, understand and communicate the mystery of life as we live it. Telling our stories and listening to the stories of others is the foundation of all culture, and healthy societies recognise the need for safe spaces where this story-telling can occur. Sadly, safe spaces to tell your story of suicidal thoughts are very rare in Australian society. On the contrary, there are far more spaces where it is distinctly dangerous to share such special and tender feelings. To change this we need first to ask the question, 'What is it like to be suicidal?', and then create the spaces where these stories can be told safely.

Later in this book a paradox surfaces that might seem to contradict my enthusiasm for story-telling. A time will come on the spiritual path when all stories must stop, if only for the briefest of moments. For me, this moment marked the end of my suicidal struggle. The spiritual silence at the end of all stories was where I finally met myself for the first time and discovered peace and freedom, and my suicidality became absurd. But to reach this moment, the stories must be told, so before we get to this silence and my own story of recovery, some other, more difficult, stories need to be told.

3

The Drug Addiction Detour

You can't heal it if you can't feel it.
Heard at an Alcoholics Anonymous meeting

In reaching out to my sister for help, both my suicidality and heroin use became public knowledge. Prior to this, I think I had been pretty successful in concealing the depths to which I had sunk ... even from myself, perhaps. But there was no hiding from it now. I was a mess. Over the next few days and weeks more and more people would learn of this. Although those closest to me have always given me fantastic support and never damned me for my behaviour, it is still very uncomfortable to raise the white flag and admit that your life is out of control and that you don't know what to do about it.

Worse than this, the most visible action I'd taken to help with my pain was to take refuge in heroin, which was perceived as overwhelmingly stupid, creating massive problems of its own. I'm sure some people thought that it was weak or self-indulgent of me to retreat into the heroin, but this was never said directly to me. These good people all wanted to look for constructive ways forward rather than to lay any guilt trips on me. Another popular view that I did hear later on, from a drug counsellor no less, was that it was 'just' my drug addiction resurfacing again, even after all these years. This is the old 'once an addict, always an addict' theory. Along with other prejudices about my drug use, this theory was to become a big part of my life for the next four years.

The consensus of those I sought help from was that I first had to attend to my drug problem, that I was never going to be able to sort out the deeper issues if I was constantly escaping from them with heroin. This made a lot of sense and was obvious really, even to me. Except that it would take nearly four years for me to finally learn that I was *never* going to get past my drug problem if the deeper issues around my suicidality were not resolved.

My first ever 'detox' was at a drug and alcohol unit in Geelong that was recommended by a friend of my sister who worked in the field. The word 'detox' here means at a detoxification centre - I had, of course, 'detoxed' (i.e. gone through the heroin withdrawals) many times by myself. This unit had a ten-day, live-in program, which is more than enough time for the physical withdrawal from heroin. It was a 'lock-up' centre in the sense that we weren't allowed out of the centre at all in these ten days for any reason, except for the daily, supervised walks. It was not a lock-up, however, in the sense that we could leave any time we wanted ... but we would not be allowed back in if we did.

It had a daily program that was carefully designed to help with the detox - routines for diet, exercise, sleep etc. - as well as classes and group therapy sessions. It was a 'non-medicated' detox, meaning that no drugs are used at all to soften the withdrawal symptoms. No pain-killers, no sleeping pills, and certainly no use at all of our drugs of abuse for a 'step-by-step' withdrawal from them. It was a 'cold turkey' detox. For this reason, people with addictions to the benzos, such as Valium, were not accepted into this unit, as these drugs require a gradual withdrawal to prevent the real risk of seizure if you try to withdraw cold turkey.

The unit could accommodate about ten people at a time and was staffed around the clock. When you first arrived, you met the others, some of whom were soon to leave and were looking pretty healthy and sharp. These 'old-timers' are important allies for the newcomers as they not only know the ropes but also typically take us newbies under their wing to help us through the first few, difficult days. A peer support culture is deliberately encouraged and is an integral, though mostly informal, part of the program. Many people who have been through detoxes speak of these relationships with other residents as the most valuable part of the whole detox process. After completing the ten days I felt 'clean' and healthy and positive again, and that it was an excellent service that had been very useful for me. I remember this place fondly, and was saddened to hear that it had been closed down for lack of funds a couple of years later.

Although I walked out of there 'clean', healthy and positive, I still picked up the heroin again the day after I left. This probably seems complete madness to those unfamiliar with addiction, but it's an all-too-common story. Very few people give up their drugs forever after their first detox. When I first contacted the unit they assumed that, at age 40, I was an old hand at the detox circuit and were surprised that this would be my first institutionalised detox. Most people my age with a heroin problem also had a history of detox visits. This was recognised, understood and accepted. It seems that, like everything else, giving up drugs takes practice. And these centres do not judge you negatively for making (yet) another attempt to give the drugs up. On the contrary, you are welcomed and congratulated for having another try and, yes, we all hope this one might prove more lasting. This is a very realistic and sensible attitude.

It was at this first detox that I also had my first encounter with Alcoholics Anonymous (AA) and its 'sister' fellowship for drug users, Narcotics Anonymous (NA). This was a big eye-opener for me. What struck me most of all at first was the scorching honesty of the stories that are told at these meetings. Extraordinary stories of struggle and recovery (though sometimes just struggle without much recovery) often told with an almost brutal frankness. Some folk 'share' their stories with a tremendous eloquence that could bring you to tears, or, just as likely, make you holler with laughter at the most awful experiences. But to 'share' at a meeting is not about eloquence or telling a good story, even though these are appreciated. Equally if not more important are the many clumsy, confused, inarticulate mumblings or ramblings of those still trying to find their own voice for their struggles with the drugs. So along with the extraordinary stories, what struck me was the incredibly genuine, attentive respect that was given to every 'share', no matter how inarticulate, angry, tear-soaked, confused or incomprehensible it might be. The feeling was very much that we were all in this together.

Over the next four years I found myself in numerous other drug and alcohol treatment places. These included short, intensive, medicated detoxes in several hospitals, as well as a couple of longer term 'rehabs'. A distinction is made between detox centres, such as my first at Geelong, and longer-term rehabilitation centres. These 'rehabs' focus more on the larger issues around establishing a lasting recovery, rather than just the initial physical detox from the drugs. For some people, just breaking the cycle of the physical addiction, perhaps supported by family, friends and/or local community services, might be sufficient to establish a strong recovery. But for many, a longer, more intensive rehabilitation is necessary. Most people with a drug addiction history will tell you that the physical addiction, strong though it might be, is actually relatively minor compared to the psychological addiction that keeps bringing us back to the drugs even after quite long periods of sobriety or staying 'clean'. The rehabs seek to address these deeper, psychological issues, which invariably takes much longer than the 'simple' physical detox. My old running coach when I was a lad used to tell me it takes as long to get fit as it took to get unfit. Getting 'straight' is a bit like this.

I went to two rehabs during my time on the drug addiction circuit. The first was a five-week program at a rehab attached to a hospital on the outskirts of Melbourne. The other was at The Buttery in rural New South Wales, which had a minimum three months' program, though it often became six months or more for many. I lasted three weeks at the hospital rehab and just three days at The Buttery.

The hospital rehab was rather posh, very intensive and very expensive. The program included daily group therapy sessions, lectures, videos and seminars on a range of topics. There were about fifteen residents at varying stages of the program, and, once again, the old-timers were a vital support for the newbies. We slept in beds in the hospital wards where there were round-the-clock nursing staff; a necessary measure, as this program included support for a medicated detox for those who needed it, though cold turkey was the preferred approach for most drugs, including heroin. Diet and exercise were important parts of the program, with fabulous vegetarian meals in the hospital dining room (but a very carnivorous BBQ on Sundays, when family could visit). It was a strictly controlled environment, including not being allowed out unless supervised. It was the 'top shelf' of rehabs, and I would not have been able to afford it without the private health insurance that I still had at the time.

I have many stories from the three, intensive weeks I spent at this place. You meet an extraordinarily mixed bag of people in these places, whom I mostly found interesting and sometimes fascinating, though not without the occasional tensions. I especially remember a lovely, devoutly religious, young woman who had never taken an intoxicating drug in her life, but had found herself seriously addicted to Valium because of a negligent doctor. She helped me to accept a genuine compliment of appreciation, which I'm still not very good at, but better than I used to be. I had simply assisted her back to her room one day when she was feeling wobbly on her feet. When she thanked me I dismissed it as nothing, but she demanded (commanded?) that I accept her thanks. I had gone the extra yard for her and she wanted me to acknowledge her appreciation. She was almost cross at me for dismissing her thanks. Her insistence forced me to pause a moment and allow myself to truly feel her appreciation. It felt great.

I joined in fully with the program, working hard to get whatever I could out of it. But I was also confused and angry and very disappointed with myself that it had come to this. In the group therapy sessions, we talked about many things - our families and other significant relationships, our work and other activities, our anger, sadness, grief, loneliness etc., as well as more specifically drug-related issues. I shared my past history with the group, mentioning that I'd been having suicidal feelings again recently.

After one of these sessions I was called into the office of the head of the unit. Our group facilitator had obviously reported to him and he told me in no uncertain terms that I was to stop talking about suicide because 'it was bullshit, just a cry for help, and it was freaking out the girls in the group'. He told me to focus on my real problem, which was my drug addiction. I was dumbstruck by this. I thought I was doing what I was meant to be doing. I felt that I was now being censored in what I could and couldn't talk about. When I told my sister about this on the phone that evening, she was clearly alarmed as she knew how I might react to this - i.e. that I might feel I needed to prove my suicidality by demonstrating it. She was relieved when I told her that I had decided to stick with the program and try and fit in with it as best I could, because I thought it was a good program and I felt it was helping.

I was to have another major conflict with the head of this unit. Part of the program was to look at our entire drug use, not just our preferred 'drug of choice'. This includes alcohol, tobacco, tea and coffee and also any prescribed medications. This guy was concerned about my alcohol drinking and the message was clear that I would have to give this up entirely too if I was to have any hope of giving up the heroin. I queried this, as I had never been a very heavy drinker and if anything my alcohol consumption in the preceding ten years or so had reduced considerably. I very rarely got drunk, certainly never had blackouts or other major symptoms of alcoholism, and was quite capable of putting half a bottle of wine back in the fridge. I virtually never drank over lunch as I used to sometimes, for the simple reason that I didn't like feeling 'groggy' in the afternoons. I really didn't see that my drinking was a significant problem.

But I listened to what these experts were trying to teach me and examined my drinking habits very carefully. My questioning of what I was being taught was seen as that great demon of recovery, denial. This demon of denial is the first and often the biggest obstacle to recovery, and has to be confronted firmly. But there is a difference between being firm, or showing 'tough love', and being a bully. This guy was a bully, though I was not aware of it at first. He was basically demanding that I accept what he was saying even though it didn't make sense to me. I was being treated as a disobedient child who had to agree with what he said 'or else'. This meant, of course, that I could pretend to agree with what he said, which would have been easy for me to do and for him to believe, but I could not take part in such a lie, which seemed to me to contradict the whole therapy process. Finally he confronted me with his 'or else' when he demanded that I kowtow to his authority or leave the unit. It was now an untenable situation for me so I had to leave.

This was very sad for me, indeed quite distressing, as I felt I was in many other ways making good progress with the program. I was consoled by my fellow residents who were concerned that leaving the unit under these circumstances would lead to my picking up the heroin again – which was exactly what happened. But I was not given much time for these consolations, as these occasions when someone is evicted are known to sometimes upset the residents that remain, and often someone who might be wavering in their commitment to the program will discharge themselves at times like this. I was frogmarched out of the unit immediately, not even allowed a phone call to find out where I might be able to stay that night. This 'boot camp' mentality is often found in detoxes and rehabs, and to some extent is perhaps necessary, given the difficult behaviours, especially around denial, that are frequent in such places. But it didn't work for me.

I don't disagree with these addiction recovery experts about the need to look at all mood-altering drugs, not just your favourite 'drug of choice'. I have met too many people for whom an abstinence from all such drugs is an essential plank of their staying sober/clean. It is very common, and makes a lot of sense, that while we may have our preferred drugs, we often use other drugs in addictive ways, particularly if our preferred drug is unavailable or hard to get. But I could not see this in my use of alcohol, which was interpreted as denial. I'd like to tell the head of this rehab today that although it's more than ten years since I last used heroin, I have been drinking alcohol, in moderation and without any urge to pick up the heroin again, even when I found myself living next door to a heroin dealer!

I must briefly mention The Buttery, the other long-term rehab I tried but where I lasted only three days. The Buttery has an excellent and well-deserved reputation, as far as I can tell. It was very different from the posh hospital rehab I'd been at a year or so previously, not least because it is affordable for those unemployed or on a pension as I was by then. It was very difficult to get into, as the demand was much greater than they could meet. But I persisted and was eventually accepted. They did not have the facilities for the detox phase of withdrawals so they required medical proof that you were 'clean' before they would admit you. This makes good sense beyond just the extra resources that are required to supervise a detox. The cultural environment created by people going through the physical and emotional intensity of detox is very different from the culture you want for the rehab phases of recovery. For instance, people who are still getting established in their recovery do not need people around them who are having major drug withdrawals with all the frustration, anger and doubts (denial) that often come with this. Being around people who are detoxing from recent drug use can also trigger the urge for a 'taste' of your old drug again.

The main reason that I fled The Buttery after just three days was simply that I was so burned out and desperate that I just didn't feel I could do it. But there were a couple of significant incidents that occurred in those few days.

First, The Buttery sends newcomers to a local GP in the first day or so for a full medical. Very sensible. When I told this GP of my history of my suicidal feelings, he recommended that I see a psychiatrist and, with my permission, he would notify The Buttery and arrange a referral. Again, very sensible, and I agreed to this. Unlike the boss at the hospital rehab in Melbourne, The Buttery understood that drug addiction might not be the sole issue that needed attention, and were sensible enough to call upon expertise other than their own, if it was needed. Big brownie points to The Buttery for this.

They lost these brownie points, however, when I met the worker who had been assigned as my counsellor. I don't know if it was Buttery policy or just this fellow's 'initiative' but he urged, almost pleaded with me, that if I was going to kill myself would I please not do it while a resident of The Buttery. I can understand his concern. It would be a big problem for them if a resident died, especially by suicide. But it did little to make me feel welcome. I felt he was more concerned about his workplace than he was about me. I assured him that I would leave first.

Both the hospital rehab in Melbourne and The Buttery advocated the AA/NA program, with residents attending local meetings as well as holding their own in-house meetings. Although it is best known for its twelve-step program, this is not the real foundation of AA/NA. The real heart and soul of AA/NA is the 'fellowship' that assembles for meetings. Before being introduced to the twelve steps, you will first and foremost be encouraged to just attend the meetings to listen to the 'sharing' of others. The wisdom and healing power of this sharing is both simple and deeply mysterious. You will be urged to look for the similarities, not the differences, between your own story and the many others you will hear, some of which might horrify you, others of which might strike you as pathetic. It's easy to find differences, which can tempt you into thinking that your situation is different, that *you* are different, that you don't really belong there. Aaah, that old demon denial is always lurking.

The first time you share you will probably be, like me, shit-scared. All these people looking at you, attending to your every word. And you're feeling lousy, confused and bewildered, not really wanting to be there and certainly not wanting to be standing before all these people wondering 'what the hell am I going to say?' But you learn pretty quickly that you can actually say any damn thing at all. It really doesn't matter. No matter how big a sweat you break into, no matter how stupid or incoherent you feel you sound, no matter how angry or sad you are feeling, whatever you say will be listened to respectfully. Here is a place where you can be yourself - with all your confusion and frustration, all your emotional dramas, all your crazy thoughts and uncertainties. Here is a place where all of you - all of you! - can be present and welcomed.

There are a few rules for meetings, known as the Twelve Traditions. The most important of these is found in the name of the fellowship, which is the right to be anonymous and the obligation to respect the anonymity of others. I see this as one of several moments of genius by the founders of AA. You could fully be yourself at meetings, but you could also create an entirely fictitious character for yourself if you wanted. Yes, this means that you could lie when you shared if you wanted to. And people often did. One of the most moving shares that I witnessed was when one fellow told the meeting that he had been lying to us all for the last few months, that he had in fact still been using, when he was telling us that he wasn't. He was in tears as he told us this. But the response of the meeting was to hold this man even closer to their hearts. Sure, we had been deceived by him, but now he had realised, as we all do eventually, that in deceiving we are really only deceiving ourselves. This moment of confessional honesty was moving and potent, and we all felt that it was potentially a very big step towards his recovery. In the tea-and-bikkies afterwards he got many hugs. There was not a trace of any negative judgement for his past deceit.

I stopped going to meetings not because of any doubts about the program but because it can, for some, become its own obstacle to recovery. Initially I didn't clearly see the reasons for this. I found that sometimes I would turn up, clean and in a good mood, only to find myself being deeply affected by some of the anger or sadness at the meeting. It was disconcerting to find myself walking away from these meetings feeling angry or upset. It was even more disconcerting when I found myself heading straight to a dealer after a meeting. This happened a couple of times and alarmed me. I learned that I had to choose the meetings I attended carefully. Each meeting has its own culture and 'personality' - some meetings seem to attract a pretty rough and angry crowd while others have a softer, more thoughtful mood. This cultural diversity, which is constantly shifting as members come and go, is a strength that reflects the broad community of the fellowship. But you need to learn which meetings can help you and which might press the wrong buttons for you and are best avoided.

But the final reason why I left and am no longer part of the AA/NA fellowship is that I found that I had never thought about drugs so much as when I was attending meetings regularly. Admittedly these were noble, hopeful, staying clean kinds of thoughts rather than the desperate, craving thoughts that I have when I'm hungry for heroin. But my heroin use had always been pretty intermittent, and when I wasn't using I was not really thinking about it that much. But to stay clean using the AA/NA program, I had to be thinking about my drug use virtually every day, which annoyed me. Again, like the 'total abstinence from all mood-altering drugs' philosophy, I have complete respect for those for whom this approach works, which it does for many. But not for me.

It was to be a year or more before I really understood why I had to leave AA/NA. And a gruesome year it was. This most awful part of my story - the 'mental illness' story - is the next chapter. But one part of this horrible year was the medical treatment I received for my heroin addiction, which belongs here in this detour into drug abuse and addiction therapy.

I had been invited to consider Methadone a couple of times but had always declined it. I didn't really know much about it, but the word 'on the street' was that it was an awful drug, as it is much more addictive than heroin and it also chains you to whoever dispenses your daily dose. Both of these are true. But finally, in mid-1998, after my first serious suicide attempt (since 1979, that is), I relented and decided to go on the Methadone. By this time I was already on anti-depressants and also an anti-psychotic drug, which we'll meet in the next chapter. I was utterly exhausted, totally lost in my helplessness and without a clue about what to do. I surrendered to the Methadone, clutching at it as a last straw.

The Methadone experiment was a failure. But unlike my experience with the psycho-drugs, I feel no resentment whatsoever towards the doctor who put me on it. This is because it clearly was an experiment and he explicitly said so. He went to great lengths to ensure that I was well informed about this drug and how the experiment might unfold. At no stage did he deceive me or make unrealistic, unjustified or extravagant promises about this drug. The idea was to create some stability in my life by managing my heroin addiction with a supervised supply of another opiate, Methadone, while I sorted things out - a reasonable approach that does work for some people. I entered into this experiment with both eyes open, well informed about the options, the risks, my own obligations, as well as the possible benefits this drug treatment *might* offer me.

I took the Methadone for about eight months, diligently visiting the chemist each day for my daily dose. As an opiate like heroin, Methadone simply substitutes one opiate addiction for another, but with three 'side effects'. First, you don't get 'high' from the Methadone itself. Some folk inject Methadone (there is a black market for it if there's a heroin drought) to get a bit of a high, but I never used it this way. Second, if you do take some heroin then it has little effect as you are already saturated with opiates. And third, it takes an awfully long time to detox from Methadone, meaning that you can't easily use it to tide you over between fixes of heroin during a drought, as it takes too long and is too painful to withdraw from.

The eight months taking these three prescribed drugs became a nightmare, mostly because of the two psycho-drugs, but the Methadone played a part. I dutifully took them all and was soon chronically constipated (probably the Methadone); became a couch-potato with a craving for ice-cream (the anti-psychotic); and had problems sleeping and was sexually inert (the anti-depressant). I didn't go out other than to get my Methadone, and was dull and uninterested in pretty much everything. And I put on about twenty kilos. Despite this, almost everyone was pretty pleased with this 'result' as I was not taking heroin and not actively suicidal. But not me. After eight months I'd had enough.

This prescribed drug-induced nightmare came to an end with my last serious suicide attempt in February 1999. This time I tried to overdose using the Methadone. Once you've been on the program for a while you're allowed the occasional take-away dose so that you don't have to go to the chemist every single day. I'd been stashing these away so that I had about fifteen doses in a bottle. My case manager had told me about a person who had died taking triple their normal dose of Methadone so I figured it would be a sure thing. I added a bottle of scotch, all the prescription drugs I had, and yes, some heroin, to make sure. I woke up with the motel staff banging on my door, dazed but otherwise still very alive. Dammit!

What do you do when you wake up to a day you never expected to have? There really is no sense of failure quite like failing at suicide. My previous serious attempts had all landed me in hospital, unconscious, where I didn't have to do anything but be a patient. I drove around for a while until I eventually (sensibly?) phoned the drug and alcohol clinic, who anxiously called me in for a medical checkup. After the doctors gave me the physical OK, I was asked to see the psychiatrist who, after a tricky interview, certified me and I was sent under guard to the Royal Park psychiatric lock-up - the details of this story are told in the next chapter.

After being discharged from Royal Park only a couple of days later, and finding and settling into somewhere new to live, I decided I was not going to take any more of these horrible drugs. I made an appointment to see my Methadone doctor, the doctor I most trusted and still have enormous respect for. Before I spoke he told me that they had reviewed my file and decided that my treatment plan was not working for me. I chuckled and agreed, telling him that I had come to a similar conclusion. I wanted to get off the psycho-drugs most of all but was advised that I should go off them one at a time, and that Methadone should be the first. Reluctantly, I accepted this argument.

Detoxing from Methadone is awful. The joke among heroin users is that nobody gets off Methadone without using heroin to help them through the Methadone withdrawals. I'm sure there are some exceptions to this street wisdom, but I was not one. The doctor put in a schedule with the chemist where I would taper off over three months. I later learned from another doctor who was to supervise this detox that this was in fact a fairly rapid schedule for the dose I was on. This new doctor actually thought it was too quick and altered it without telling me. When I became aware of this deception I was outraged and insisted that we return to the original schedule. I was keen to get off the Methadone so I could then get off the other, wretched psycho-drugs.

As I worked through this detox schedule, which I was doing 'blind', meaning that I was not told when the dose was reduced, the chemist asked me a few times whether I'd 'hit the wall' yet. He was referring to the full-blast of Methadone withdrawal symptoms, which almost always came, though at unpredictable times in the process. I kept saying no ... until the very last week of the schedule. I staggered in there one day and told him the wall had come - aches, cold sweats, limp with fatigue, craving some sort of 'relief'. At these times it is recommended that you stop any further dose reductions, maybe even return to a higher dose, until you stabilise for a while and then resume the schedule. I was down to some tiny dose and due to have my last ever dose the next Friday. I decided, after speaking with the chemist and my doctor, that I would tough it out, pretend that I was sick with the flu or something for a while, and proceed to my final dose on the Friday. The next six weeks were just awful, and I did take some heroin a couple of times to help. But I've not taken any since then.

Without telling my doctors, I had already stopped taking the psycho-drugs by this time. I can clearly recall the time when I went to take the anti-psychotic tablet and just couldn't bring myself to put it in my mouth. Never again.

Today, with the hindsight of what is now a robust recovery, I can see that I was never going to get over my addiction to heroin while my internal, suicidal despair was still brewing inside me. The focus on my 'drug problem' was a massive distraction that dominated my four years of madness. While I was being taught - and tried hard to believe - that I was an 'addict', everyone's attention, including mine, was not looking at the real issues. I still treasure my encounter with AA/NA, which I would readily recommend to anyone struggling with addictions. I must also acknowledge the genuine efforts of some of the doctors in my struggle with heroin. But in the end these addiction therapies, like the drug abuse itself, were a detour from the path I would have to walk if I was ever going to recover from my suicidal despair.

* * * * *

I include this chapter about my drug history with some reluctance and hesitation. Not because I'm ashamed or embarrassed about it – I'm not, or not much (though nor am I proud of it). Nor because it's such a complex, controversial and emotive issue, with strong feelings on both sides of the 'drug debate'. No, I hesitate to dwell on my drug history because it's a distraction from understanding suicide as a crisis of the self, which is the essential story of this book.

But I must include it because it was a significant part of my suicidal struggle for four years. With hindsight, I can perhaps acknowledge that it was a necessary detour, as a stepping-stone to my eventual recovery. I just wish this detour hadn't taken four years. It is also relevant because the struggle with addictions can point to some core issues around suicide, mental health in general, and the self-enquiry and spirituality that are the major themes of this book. In particular, the genius of the founders of Alcoholics Anonymous contains vital insights into recovery (including the concept of recovery itself), insights that the mental health industry we meet in the next chapter is only just beginning to wake up to.

The first and most important of these is the need for *a safe space to tell your story*, such as the fellowship meetings of AA/NA. The importance of this cannot be overstated. Equally, the lack of safe story-telling spaces in our culture and communities is a social crisis that also cannot be overstated. The healing of any personal crisis of the self always begins with telling your story. Perhaps most important of all are the stories we tell ourselves, our self-talk stories; and sometimes, perhaps most of the time, this is sufficient by itself for the healing that we need. But these stories can also be part of the crisis if they are confused or wounded stories, as is often the case with memories of past pains or fears of uncertain futures. Sometimes we need help with the telling of our stories.

This might include the help of a professional counsellor, which we will look at in the next chapter. But for now we just note that any counselling always begins with the telling of your story and that much of the counselling process aims to 're-write' these stories so that they don't cause so much pain. Before seeking professional help, though, we will probably share our stories with family and friends. The healing that comes from this is often just the sharing of the story itself and not necessarily the advice we might receive from these friends. What we most need when we share these stories is an attentive listener, which I sometimes call 'honest listening'. More recently I have come to recognise this honest listening in the beautiful phrase 'to bear witness', in particular to bear witness to another's suffering.

One of the essential features of this 'honest listening' is first to accept the person *as they are*. None of us can ever truly know the reality of any other. To accept a person as they are, without judgement, is to respect their reality, no matter how chaotic, confused or incomprehensible it may seem. Sometimes another person's stories may resonate with us, and we experience an immediate *empathy* with them. At other times this empathy will be weak or absent and we are face to face with the mystery of another person's reality. Skilful, honest listeners will recognise the differences between these occasions, and will not feign empathy when none exists. This is so important because few things are more frustrating – and less therapeutic – than false empathy.

This honest listening is vital not only for empathy. It allows 'all of me' to be present in any conversation or dialogue. This all-of-me, even if I am not particularly in touch with myself at times, is the me, the self that is in crisis during suicidal despair. My suicidal feelings often included a peculiar feeling of being invisible. Little did I realise that it was actually my being invisible to myself that was at the core of this. But so often I also felt invisible, or only partially visible, when I sought treatment. That is, I felt that only certain parts or aspects of me were visible to the counsellor/therapist. Sometimes this was not so serious, and maybe even necessary in order to focus on specific issues, but at other times the very narrow perceptions and prejudices of the therapist were harmful, even abusive. We will meet examples of this in the next chapter.

Of all the professional counsellors, doctors, psychologists and other therapists that I encountered during my four years of madness, there was only one, a woman called Nicky, with whom I truly felt that all-of-me was always allowed to be fully present. This is not to say that Nicky saw and empathised fully with all of me all the time. Nicky simply allowed all of me to be present in all its confusion and mystery. What she couldn't see or couldn't comprehend was still invited into our sessions together. Whatever arose could always be acknowledged, and then sometimes discussed, debated, even contradicted and argued against. But never banished. Another way of saying it is to say that no part of me was denied a presence with Nicky. This was truly great 'honest listening'.

In order to tell our stories, with all-of-me fully present, we need a space that is *safe*. If we are in crisis then we are unlikely to be forthcoming with our stories unless we feel it is safe to do so. With suicidal stories this is particularly acute because of the shame, fear, ignorance and prejudices – the toxic and very unsafe taboos – that we know will likely be present if we attempt a conversation about our suicidal feelings. All of me cannot be present when the biggest issue on my mind at the time, my suicidal thoughts, are denied, rejected or avoided. If we detect this occurring, then we will quite likely retreat further into the 'closed world of the suicidal mind' and withhold our stories – and the crisis deepens. There are very few safe spaces where we can talk about suicidal thoughts.

One particularly hazardous space is the one-on-one, behind-closed-doors space that is the typical therapeutic space adopted by many counsellors. In this space, another individual, who we do not really know at all, enters our private and often secret worlds at a time when we are particularly vulnerable. This is an inherently risky space. We would like to trust the professional qualifications of these people and believe that it is safe to tell them our stories. But if all of me is not allowed into this space by the therapist – who owns control of this space in a very unequal relationship – then this secretive, closed space can be very dangerous indeed (as we will see in the next chapter).

A *safe space to tell your story* is the very foundation of AA/ NA. It exists in the meetings of the fellowship. The genius of its founders recognised that 'sharing' was in itself healing, and that anonymity helps to create a safe space where all of you – all of me and all of us – can be present. The culture of these meetings is that we do not judge or advise others when they share – we just listen. Honest listening. We learn to listen – to bear witness – with an honest, open ear and an honest, open heart. Empathy naturally arises in this space, but there is also no room in this space for false empathy. Along with the sensitivity that comes from recognising mutually shared problems comes a ruthless honesty that does not allow artificial pretences for very long. This space also has the safety of numbers. There are no closed-door, secret, one-on-one relationships with all the hazards of the 'transference' and 'counter-transference' that counsellors seem to make so much of. The many heads and hearts at an AA/NA meeting, moreover, bring a richness of culture that is impossible in a private consultation between two individuals. Being in a group of your peers also acknowledges your pain and struggle when you recognise that you are not altogether alone, that others have been here in this space before you and are with you now. As well as a safe space, it is also an inherently destigmatising environment. You learn that you do not have to suffer in solitude (unless you choose to), and the toxic loneliness becomes a little less lonely and a little less toxic.

Another feature of AA/NA is its twelve-step program, and in particular that it is an unabashedly spiritual program. For some reason this causes much confusion and prejudice about AA/NA, especially among its critics. The key to this spirituality, however, is simply to acknowledge some Higher Power greater than your individual self, and to look to this for guidance in your struggle against addiction. This is all the spirituality that the program speaks of. They do use the word 'God', which can be an obstacle for many, including me, but it can be whatever you want it to be. Some people see it as a religious God, others see it as Mother Nature, still others relate to this notion best as some form of Higher Self. There are many ways of approaching this Higher Power or Spirit.

Entering into relationship with this Higher Power, and humbly acknowledging our own failures, we are invited to 'surrender' to this power. This surrender is definitely not the 'giving up' that would probably lead us back to our drugs (or suicide). Nor is it a blind-faith belief in some supernatural father figure or religious doctrine. It is an opening up to the deeper mystery of life. It is to let go of and transcend our attachment to the self-centred ego of the mind and all the battles we have with this ego. It is an invitation to allow into our lives a power and an experience that comes from beyond the individual self. If we dare to accept this invitation then many of us find ourselves in the embrace of a mysterious, loving and healing universe or spirit – a universe from which we all arose and of which we are all part. This is the Spirit (or Higher Power or God) that breathes life into us all, and can, if we allow it, lead us to recovery. From our addictions. And, for some, from our suicidal despair.

One other acknowledgement I would like to make to the founders of AA/NA is that they pioneered the notion of 'recovery' from addiction, and in particular that recovery is possible for everyone, without exception. Furthermore, recovery is not seen narrowly in terms of just physical health or the absence of illness. Recovery takes into account the whole person – body, mind and spirit – and also our relationships with family, friends and community. Recovery is more holistic, being concerned with the whole of our being and our personal sense of well-being. It does not assume that healing is necessarily about eradicating disease and is not as 'treatment' oriented as the medical approach. Recovery can mean becoming intimate with your suffering and learning from it, growing into a greater fullness, a more complete sense of wholeness and a deeper experience of life. Recovery emphasises personal growth rather than illness.

I am amazed at some of the criticisms made of Alcoholics Anonymous. The most common one is that it replaces an addiction to alcohol or drugs with an addiction to religion, which is then put down as blind faith in a supernatural deity or religious dogma. First of all, this is far from the spirituality of AA/NA (or this book). But even if this were so, I am stunned that these critics put such an addiction in the same class as drug addiction. Even if it is such a simplistic spiritual addiction, is this not vastly superior to the drug addictions that brought us to AA/NA? At meetings you will hear many stories of sickness, crime, cheating on friends and families, poverty, and waking up in the gutter in a pile of your own vomit. You will also hear many stories of people who, having embraced the 'addiction' to their Higher Power have restored their physical health, repaired broken relationships, resumed work or studies, and now have hope and possibilities in their future. And yet the critics somehow regard these 'addictions' as comparable.

There are other criticisms about AA/NA, such as its use of the 'disease model of addiction' that you will find mentioned at meetings. I share this criticism, except that my understanding is that this model is not in fact part of the AA program or philosophy but has somehow seeped into AA/NA over the years. The disease model says that addiction is a disease, in particular a disease of the brain, which, furthermore, is a progressive and incurable disease. There is also the implication that this disease is genetic, at least partially, so that once it's triggered by taking drugs or alcohol, you will then have the disease for life. Once an addict, always an addict. I was taught this model of addiction at some of the detoxes and rehabs I went to, and tried hard to accept that it was true and that I had this disease. But in the end I simply couldn't, which the same model then interprets as denial. This model explains the bullying behaviour of the boss of the Melbourne hospital rehab who viewed this disease as my 'real problem', and my inability to find addictive behaviour in my drinking as merely a symptom of my denial of this disease.

I hesitate to completely damn the disease model for a couple of reasons. The first is that there is no doubt that there are some biological factors in a person's *susceptibility* to addiction. Some people seem to drink and drug heavily for years without falling into serious addiction problems, while others seem to fall into it almost from the very beginning of their drinking and drugging career. But this is not sufficient to call it solely a biological disease. We will meet this sort of folly again when we look at 'mental illness', but the obsession with looking only to biology as the sole source of various behaviours fails to consider our psychological, social and spiritual needs. There is a saying that if the only tool you have is a hammer then everything looks like a nail. I once translated this for one of my doctors, who saw psychology in mainly biochemical terms, 'if the only knowledge you have is biochemistry then everything looks biochemical'. This narrow, shallow and simplistic ignorance of the full depth of the psyche, in all its mystery and subtlety, has become an arrogant and harmful pathologising in modern medicine, especially in psychiatry.

Another reason I hesitate is that I have met many people who have taken great comfort from learning that their addictions were a biological disease. This might seem odd at first, to be grateful to learn that you have a progressive, incurable disease, but for many it truly is a great relief. Again, there are many parallels here with the medicalisation of 'mental illness'. For those of us who struggle with these difficulties – either addiction or madness – it is easy to feel that it is because of some terrible character flaw or that we are in some way 'bad' people. The pain we suffer and the troubles we get into undermine our sense of self and lead to a deep sense of failure. It can be reassuring, indeed a great relief, to learn that you have a disease and that your suffering is due to some biological malfunction – that it's not *your* fault. This can help us let go of our self-blame, shame, and feelings of personal failure. And from this starting point, we can often proceed with recovery.

So it is with some hesitation, and even some sadness, that I have to say that the comfort we get from this 'diagnosis' is in fact based on a false belief. For many people, their path to recovery commenced when they got a diagnosis based on the disease model, so it seems unfair, almost cruel, to challenge it and undermine this seemingly therapeutic intervention as a false belief. My 'bottom line' for any therapy is whether it works; so if people are liberated from their suffering by false beliefs then that's fine with me. But only up to a point, because these false beliefs – unlike the truth – can also be harmful. When the boss at the Melbourne hospital rehab bullied me with his belief in the disease model, this was abuse, and potentially dangerous abuse. Similar abuses based on similar false beliefs are now widespread in modern psychiatry.

Another criticism, more of spirituality in general rather than AA/NA specifically, is that it is escapism. This has some parallels with the 'substitute addiction' criticism, but is an intriguing perspective to explore for the questions it raises about our sense of self. Drug use itself can be seen as a form of escape, sometimes called 'self-medicating', which was certainly true of my use of heroin. I used it to escape the pain of being me. Such escapism is commonly seen in fairly derogatory terms, but we all 'escape' from our lives regularly, in many different ways. We 'escape' when we take a holiday or go to the movies, or perhaps through adventure sports or other pastimes. We 'escape' through a whole variety of drugs, some of which are legally and/or culturally endorsed. We 'escape' into a different reality through the great spiritual contemplative traditions of prayer or meditation. And each night, we 'escape' into sleep, another consciousness, another reality, but unquestionably a necessary escape. Some psychologists see such escapes as essential to a healthy sense of self and something that we must all do regularly to sustain a healthy self. These essential escapes can become harmful (pathological) if indulged excessively (addictively), but they are not automatically or necessarily so. Indeed, it is argued that a life without these regular escapes will become pathological in other ways. This is an interesting and useful line of enquiry, but I won't pursue it further here, other than to pose the intriguing questions of what is it we are escaping *from* and/or what is it we are escaping *to*?

Before moving away from the drug story and on to mental health, it is worth having a brief look at the overlap between these two sectors. In recent years we have seen the emergence of what is called 'dual-diagnosis' to refer to those who have both mental health and substance abuse problems. It is now increasingly apparent that this is the case for many people, and that many of them are falling through the large gaps between the two services – especially young people. Each of these services will often refer someone with both problems to the other service, saying either that they lack the expertise to deal with the other, or that the other needs to be attended to first. This 'ping-pong' between the services is a huge gap that many people disappear into, so that they end up never receiving either service. It also indicates a deep rift between these services.

The following table sums up the major differences between mental health and drug and alcohol services. It shows that what is sometimes called 'co-morbidity' is not so much about the individual person in strife as it is about two services of very different philosophies and cultures.

My experience of both sectors tells me that the mental health sector has very much more to learn from the drug and alcohol sector than the other way round. But what is currently happening is precisely the opposite, with the increasing medicalisation of drug and alcohol services – the terminology of 'dual-diagnosis' itself indicates this. The excessive medicalisation of everyday life, which is sometimes called disease mongering, has become the medical colonisation of what it is to be human. Nowhere is this more apparent – or more harmful – than in the medicalisation of mental health.

Mental Health	Drug and Alcohol
Medical model	Psychosocial model
Focus on treatment (of illness/ symptoms)	Focus on recovery
Biological	More holistic
Pathologises the individual	Considers social context
Emphasises deficits (illness)	Strengths-based
Intimidating	Welcoming
Little or no peer support	Strong peer support
Disempowering, little patient participation of residents	Active participation
Mostly clinical staff	Mostly non-clinical staff, many of them recovered drug users
Involuntary	Voluntary

4

The 'Mental Illness' Circus

> There are some things in our social system to which I am proud to be maladjusted and to which I suggest that we ought to be maladjusted. The salvation of the world lies in the hands of the creatively maladjusted.
>
> Martin Luther King Jr.

My first encounter with mental health services (as opposed to drug addiction treatments) was with a psychiatrist, not long after I had called out to my sister for help back in late '95. He came highly recommended by someone whose opinion I trusted. I called to make an appointment and had the first of many difficult lessons in psychiatry.

The first time available to see him was something like three weeks away. But I was calling because I was scared that I might not survive the next day or so. I didn't mention this as it felt too melodramatic and pathetic and, I guess, too embarrassing to say over the phone. Full of uncertainty, I made the appointment anyway. My situation deteriorated and I was getting very frightened about my growing suicidal feelings. I was thinking about little else. One night I was feeling so distraught and unable to sleep that I called some emergency number (I don't recall which) who contacted the Crisis Assessment and Treatment (CAT) Team on my behalf.

They must have been having a quiet night because, before too long, two CAT-people turned up, a guy and a woman. I was impressed with how skilfully they handled me. They talked me down from the fear I was feeling and we discussed a strategy to get through just the next twenty-four hours. When I said I had an appointment with a psychiatrist but it was still over a week away they said they would contact him. They left saying they'd be in touch the next day and I was calmed down sufficiently to be confident that I could wait until I heard from them. Which I did, the next day as promised, when they told me they had spoken to the psychiatrist and that I had an appointment for the following day. I never saw my CAT friends again and don't remember their names. But I'm grateful for their visit that night.

The psychiatrist worked from home and he first reassured himself that I wasn't manic and didn't need any heavy sedation – I think he mentioned Lithium. We talked about anti-depressants and after the second or third session I agreed to try Aurorix, my first psycho-medication. It didn't have any noticeable effect, and we figured it was probably due to the fact that I was still using heroin pretty regularly. Another psychiatrist a year or so later referred to Aurorix as 'lollies'.

Nothing really happened during the eight to ten times that I saw this psychiatrist. He seemed to be waiting for the Aurorix to kick in, but it never did. I do recall, though, that he answered his mobile phone at least two or three times in each session I had with him. At around $120 per forty-five minute session I thought this was a bit rich, but I was too polite to have a go at him about it. My first lesson in modern psychiatry.

It was probably not long after this that I started seeing Nicky. Nicky is a very special character in this story. She is neither a psychiatrist nor a psychologist but does professional development work in the corporate world, that includes, I think, some individual counselling, plus she sees just a few private individual clients at home. I had known Nicky, a friend of my sister, for several years and it was with Nicky that I'd had some brief relationship counselling with my partner before it all fell apart. Nicky is special because, after my suicidality and heroin addiction finally passed in 1999, she was like the single thread of sanity woven through all of those four horrible years. Of all the people I sought help from, it was only with Nicky that I never, not once, felt invisible. With Nicky, all of me was always allowed to be fully present. My broken heart, my suicidality, my heroin use, my fears and doubts and pain, and also my soul and my confused and chaotic spirituality at the time – all of me was always welcomed into the sessions with Nicky even when she found aspects of this bewildering to her. Nicky has many special gifts but none greater than her generous capacity to simply 'bear witness' and be with me in my madness and to hold and embrace its chaos with respect and without judgement.

Nicky made it clear at the outset that neither drug addiction nor crisis counselling was her area of expertise. But she was willing to see me and support me as best she could while I looked for some other counselling which might be more specific to my needs. In the end, such a counsellor was never found and it was Nicky who was still there for me when freedom finally arrived nearly four years later. Despite this, Nicky would never say that she was my saviour, or that she rescued or cured me. Like me, she would see all these as silly ideas that get in the way of meaningful personal growth – call it therapy, if you must.

Apart from Nicky and that first encounter with psychiatry, the emphasis of the first year or so of 'treatment' was primarily the drug addiction detour of the previous chapter. My next encounter with psychiatry came after fleeing The Buttery, the drug rehab in northern New South Wales. After chickening out yet again on another plan to kill myself, I made my way to Port Macquarie Base Hospital, looking for a psychologist called Phil who had been recommended by a friend from nearby Wauchope. As a consulting psychologist to the hospital, Phil was not there all the time, and to see him at the hospital I first had to go through the admission assessment process of the hospital's psych unit. I don't recall whether I was actually seeking to be admitted – maybe I was. I was certainly looking for some refuge from my lost world. Anyway, I was assessed and admitted, but before eventually getting to see Phil I was seen by the psychiatrist in charge of the psych unit.

This psychiatrist immediately diagnosed me with 'depression' and recommended an anti-depressant called Aropax – this was the guy who thought the Aurorix pills I'd previously taken were 'lollies'. I was again reluctant to take anti-depressants, I think because I felt a sense of failure in resorting to the drugs, which sounds pretty silly given the state I was in and the illegal drug that I was self-medicating with. I was not vehemently opposed to them on principle, I just wanted to try and work things out without them if possible. In particular, I wanted at least to try some counselling with Phil first. This psychiatrist was clearly scornful of Phil's 'talking therapy' and I guess I reacted a bit to his pressure to take his drugs. He was quite pushy and also a pretty smug and unpleasant person, which may have influenced me too. When I finally decided not to take his drugs he in turn decided to discharge me from 'his' psych unit. But by then I had made contact with Phil and I liked him.

The few days in this psych unit (less than a week, I think it was), together with the time with Phil, managed to calm me down some so that my suicidality was not burning hot within me as it had been when I was admitted. After a short while with some local friends, I headed back to Melbourne, but I picked up the heroin again and it wasn't too long before I found myself doing another detox, this time in a private hospital. It was this detox where I first met the terrific doctor who on a later occasion put me on the Methadone. After this particular detox and with the assistance of another friend, I went to a yoga ashram in the country where I lived very happily (most of the time) and drug-free (most of the time) for the rest of that year. I'll tell some of this story in another chapter.

The story here resumes in late 1996 after I'd left the ashram to go to a spiritual retreat to hear a woman called Gangaji (who we'll meet again later in this story), in Murwillumbah. After six months in the ashram I thought I was fine, but in the couple of weeks it took me to get from the ashram to the retreat I was back on to the heroin again. It was hopeless. I was hopeless.

On the second night at this retreat, I woke up in the middle of the night silently screaming for no more of this wretched life, feeling overwhelmed with the necessity to die now, right now. I had neither a plan nor the means to kill myself, but I just wanted to die so much. All I could find in the tent with me that might possibly do the job was my razor. I had never deliberately cut myself before - this was brand new territory for me. Today I laugh at the comical side of this when I think of how unlikely it is to cut yourself to death with one of today's modern twin-blade razors. I did manage to make quite a mess of my arms, but I was never going to die this way.

When I woke up after finally collapsing from the physical and emotional exhaustion (and a little Valium), I sensibly figured that I should get some medical attention for my arms. When I showed them to the organisers of the retreat they saw immediately what had happened and gently but urgently arranged for me to go to the hospital in nearby Lismore. While waiting for assessment by the psych staff, I took off. I headed for Nimbin, determined that *this* time I would finally do it properly.

It took no time at all in Nimbin to purchase a couple of hundred dollars worth of good, strong, cheap heroin. More than enough for the task at hand. I treated myself to just a regular dose as I made preparations to take the rest in one shot. It was not the first time that the relief of the heroin high gave me pause to think again about what I was about to do. I could possibly argue that this self-medication with heroin stopped me from going ahead with my suicidal intentions on numerous occasions. Although there is certainly some truth in this, it's also true that this was not the only reason for my ambivalence. And I'd rather not endorse or encourage the use of heroin as an anti-depressant - it truly does create far more problems than it solves.

But, in this pause, I heard a voice, or perhaps I just recalled what this voice had said to me some time before. It was the voice of Phil, the psychologist from Port Macquarie. I can still vividly recall the words that came back to me in Nimbin while preparing my final hit. They were simply 'if you find yourself thinking of having a go at yourself, please come and see me first'.

It's funny what sticks in the mind or comes back to you at certain critical moments. Another similar remark was made some years later by my GP at another critical moment. He simply said, 'Please don't die'. I think the significance of these two requests came from the mutual trust and respect I had with these two guys. I could actually feel in these utterances their concern and their caring for me, something I never really felt with any of the psychiatrists I saw. I also think that these heartfelt but simple requests indicated an acknowledgement by these two guys that they both knew that ultimately they were powerless to stop me from killing myself. They both wanted to help but they also knew that in the end it was my decision, which showed an honesty and respect for me that I rarely found elsewhere, and which was really precious for me, maybe even life-saving.

When Phil's words came to me (and perhaps with the help of the heroin), I hesitated. Before long my doubts were approaching life-saving proportions. I wondered how I might get to Port Macquarie. Would I be able to find Phil? What would happen if I went, and was there any point to making such an effort? And then I realised that I couldn't go through with my suicide plan; that while there was this doubt I had to give it a chance. Aware of the finality of suicide, part of me felt that it was probably important to exhaust all possibilities before taking that final step. So, fortified with heroin,

I took a cab then a bus, then a train, to Wauchope and then the local school bus to the hospital.

I was dazed, very stoned and exhausted when I approached the psych unit and asked for Phil. The staff at the desk said that Phil was not there until later in the day, and that I would again have to be assessed by the medical staff first. It was early in the day and I was asked to wait, so I went outside to the courtyard to have a smoke. I sat there for some time, unknowingly getting quite sunburnt in my stoned daze. After a while some staff came out and started setting up the barbecue for a staff lunch. I sat there watching. Finally one of these women asked me what I was doing and I said waiting to be assessed for admission. Her face dropped as she realised they had forgotten about me.

The assessment was pretty straightforward as I was clearly in a bad way (and now sunburnt as well). Except it was pointed out to me that I would first have to do a detox in a hospital ward before going into the psych unit. This took about a week and included another of my clumsy, half-hearted and embarrassing suicide attempts, when I tried to hang myself on the shower hose in the hospital bathroom.

In the psych unit I surrendered this time to the urging of the psychiatrist to go on the anti-depressant medication. I say surrendered here quite deliberately as the first reaction to this decision, well before any effect from the drug, was that I felt some relief to have finally abandoned my own efforts to save myself. I simply had to admit that I was bewildered and failing in my own attempts to sort things out, so I surrendered myself to the advice of the experts. In a peculiar way, admitting that I really was the complete misfit that I was afraid I was actually turned out to be something of a relief. For a little while.

I spent about three weeks in the psych unit this time. This was to monitor me - i.e. keep me safe - while waiting for the Aropax to start taking effect, but also to watch for any side effects. There were no noticeable side-effects but nor was there any noticeable therapeutic effect, so the dose was increased. The psychiatrist told me that the one side-effect that people reported on this drug was that they sometimes found themselves not caring so much about some of the things they normally used to care about. I joked, 'But doc, isn't that why I'm here in the first place?'

This was my longest stay in a psych unit and one of the biggest problems in these places is how unbelievably boring it is. This is recognised by the doctors and nursing staff, but nobody does anything about it. Very occasionally one of the nurses would bring out a board game or some cards. Even less often, some pretty lame efforts were made to do activities that are supposedly therapeutic. But no one is much interested in them - including the nursing staff. The 'library' was a tiny and tattered collection of things like Readers Digest abridged versions and frayed waiting-room magazines, of which I read as much as I could stomach. Meals, TV and the medication rounds were the highlights of the day. It felt much like a child-minding centre as we sat back and waited for the drugs to do their magic. The nursing staff were as disgruntled and bored as the patients. One of them complained to me that this unit had not yet been registered to take involuntary patients and it seemed to me that he was saying that 'real' psychiatric nursing required involuntary patients.

The psychiatrist did his round of the unit each day, which meant that you had a few minutes with him where he'd maybe fine-tune your medication. And, importantly for me, I had a session with Phil every couple of days. The psychiatrist was clearly still scornful of Phil and his counselling, but now that I was being obedient and taking the medications, I was not asked to leave. After three weeks, though, it was time to go. I had calmed down considerably over this time, which the psychiatrist attributed to the anti-depressant. I didn't really feel any noticeable effect from the drug, other than a slightly stoned dullness, but I attributed most of this to the intense boredom of the place. I was ready to leave.

I decided to go and live with my friends in the forest, inland from Port Macquarie. I didn't want to live in a big city and I felt that I'd got all that I could from the ashram. I was ready to move on rather than return there. I also wanted to keep seeing Phil. So, after a trip back to Melbourne and the ashram to pack up a few of my things, I moved into the rustic but for me quite idyllic life in the hills among the trees. I spent a year here, living healthy and getting strong again. I was taking the anti-depressant medication and seeing Phil once a week in Port Macquarie.

I wanted to see Phil because I knew that my inner discontent was still far from resolved. In the peace and tranquillity of my secluded, rustic lifestyle, I was not actively suicidal, but I was aware - or at least semi-aware - that I was still hiding from a world that I did not want to be a part of. I'm sure that some people saw my apparent calming down as me finally coming to terms with the broken heart that had triggered this whole sorry saga in the first place - maybe I was simply growing out of it at last. I'm equally sure that some others, such as the psychiatrist who prescribed the anti-depressants, saw this apparent improvement as due to the medication. But I knew that I was still troubled, and hoped that I could work through some of these aching questions with Phil.

The first and most important thing about Phil was that his concern and compassion for me were evident and genuine. He was honest with me, including listening honestly without judgement, and not feigning any false empathy. A mutual trust and respect developed quite quickly between us, which remained throughout the year that I spent with him. He showed a genuine commitment to helping me, including adjusting his rates for me so that I could see him as frequently as I did. He did not pretend to have any magic wand that could cure me, but energetically applied his professional skills to help me unravel whatever it was that seemed to be haunting me. I greatly appreciate his efforts and remember that year with him fondly.

It seems to me that it should be unnecessary to highlight these admirable qualities that I found in Phil. Surely it's reasonable to expect these from anyone we approach for help with mental, emotional and/or spiritual problems. But I do feel the need to highlight the compassion, sensitivity and honesty of Phil because of the extraordinary absence of these qualities among the psychiatrists I sought help from.

I cannot say which particular school of psychology Phil practised. I now know that there are many different approaches to psychotherapy and I suspect Phil mixed together a blend of these according to what he felt might be most useful for me. Now that I'm familiar with cognitive behaviour therapy I can see that at times he was clearly working with these techniques, where we look for negative thinking patterns and try and nip them in the bud and cultivate other, more positive thoughts. This is effectively rewriting the scripts we use to respond to life's circumstances, which can be a very useful method for changing these patterns of negativity.

At other times he was clearly practising some 'depth psychology' techniques, delving into the unconscious and subconscious motivations for my behaviour, looking for the source of my pain. We also looked at my history of relationships - interpersonal therapy - with family, friends and past lovers. Much useful territory was explored.

Another important feature of Phil's professionalism became apparent when I talked with him about spirituality. First of all, he was respectful of it and in principle endorsed the legitimacy and potential benefits of the spiritual quest. But he was explicit that he was a psychologist, not a spiritual guide. He listened attentively and supportively when I talked of yoga and meditation and other aspects of my spirituality, but he rarely responded to this and certainly never gave anything that you might call spiritual advice. He was very clear about what he saw as the boundaries of his expertise and what he was able to offer in this therapeutic relationship. I admire Phil enormously for this - both for his clarity about his role and for his honesty with me about that.

But, after a year of weekly counselling sessions, we never got to the core of my despair. The last time I saw Phil must have been very sad for him. I had decided to return to Melbourne, but in just one short fortnight before leaving the district I had already picked up the heroin again and my suicidality was again percolating away inside me not far from the surface. I was clearly a mess again and Phil would have seen this. I thanked him for all his help and, with my own sadness, bade him farewell. Despite this lack of 'success', I am unable to be critical of his genuine and compassionate efforts on my behalf.

The same cannot be said for my experiences with psychiatrists. We have already met two psychiatrists in this story so far - one who answered his phone during counselling sessions, and the other who was disdainful of Phil's talking therapy. In the final year of my journey to recovery (roughly mid-'98 to mid-'99), I was to have encounters with four more psychiatrists. Two of these encounters were also brief and in some ways quite trivial, but still need to be mentioned for what they reveal. The other two I regard as significant abuses of the trust that I placed in these men when I sought their help. But first, a little more of the journey that led me to these people.

It's now early 1998 and I've left the forests of NSW and the counselling with Phil. I wanted to be at my dad's 80th birthday, but picked up a pretty full-on heroin habit on the slow road back to Melbourne. I managed to make it back in time for my dad's party, and also managed to present a reasonably calm face at this wonderful celebration. But I knew I was in trouble, so a day or so after the party I sought out the drug and alcohol doctor that I knew and liked and trusted from previous detoxes. He again suggested the Methadone and again I declined, but I did yet another hospitalised detox.

While still in hospital I saw the psychiatrist who would later certify me and send me to Royal Park after a suicide attempt. On this occasion we talked through the options and I agreed to go back on the anti-depressants again. I'd stopped taking the Aropax when I left NSW because I didn't think they were helping and I didn't like the side-effects - mainly the 'sexual dysfunction'. He may have thought that my falling into the heroin again was because of this but he was decent enough not to say so.

He suggested I try one of the newer drugs at the time, a drug called Efexor. Normally when you start on one of these drugs you begin with maybe half the recommended full dose to see if that's sufficient for you and also to see if you might have any side-effects. Given my history and my rather desperate state, this guy recommended that I start at the full adult dose, to which I agreed. After a couple of weeks there was no really noticeable therapeutic effect, but nor were there any significant side-effects. So we doubled the dose and there was an almost immediate effect. I could not sleep. After about ten days with a total of maybe ten hours sleep, I called the psychiatrist and insisted that I could not continue with this and had to see him.

We considered the possibilities. First, we could switch to another anti-depressant. It is well known that some people respond to some anti-depressants while others do not. Side-effects are also equally unpredictable. So 'shopping around' for maximum benefit and/or minimum side-effects is a common practice. He was reluctant to do this though, because there was a window of time between weaning off the current drug and the new drug kicking in, which he thought might be a risky time for me. The option he recommended was to add another chemical to my drug diet that he claimed would 'augment the anti-depressant effect' of the Efexor. He described it as a catalyst that would boost the serotonin-enhancing properties of the Efexor. This drug also had a sedative effect, which would hopefully help me to sleep. The drug was Zyprexa.

Zyprexa is an anti-psychotic drug that was developed for the treatment of psychosis and, in particular, schizophrenia. I asked the psychiatrist whether he thought I was 'psychotic' or 'schizophrenic'. He reassured me that I was not, and repeated why he felt this drug might help me - that it would augment the serotonin-boosting effect of the Efexor. When I said OK, I'll give it a go, he got on the phone for the authorisation required to claim this expensive drug on the Pharmaceutical Benefit Scheme (PBS). He gave them some details for the authorisation and then I heard him say 'schizophrenia'. After he hung up I asked what was that about? He said that the PBS expects this drug to be prescribed for schizophrenia and that it's easier to tell them what they want to hear. At the time we chuckled over this deception. But it's not so funny for me now.

I still wonder if there is a government database somewhere that has me recorded as having received treatment for schizophrenia. And if there is, what are the consequences that might possibly arise due to this wrong information? I still don't know. My GP tells me that access to the PBS database is very strictly controlled, but I'm not altogether reassured by this. I was once told that both the psychiatrist and I were guilty of defrauding the government through this deception. Maybe, but I do not accept much of the responsibility, as I feel that I myself was deceived by the psychiatrist, and far more seriously than just in cheating the government of a few dollars.

This psychiatrist deliberately and knowingly deceived me in order to get me to take this brutal, brain-numbing drug. It is simply impossible that he was not aware of the broad effect and potency of Zyprexa or of his duty to inform me about this. To present it as just some 'catalytic serotonin booster' was a gross misrepresentation of this drug, and a devious manipulation of my ignorance and vulnerability at the time. It is necessary to ask why he felt the need to resort to such a drug and such a deception. My answer is that he just didn't have a clue what to do with me - which became very clear nearly a year later when he certified me.

Although the mind-numbing 'therapeutic' effect of Zyprexa was concealed from me, he did warn me of the most common side-effect of this drug. He said I 'might develop a bit of a sweet tooth'. This proved to be quite an understatement, as I developed not so much a 'sweet tooth' but an addictive passion for ice-cream (which I usually ate only rarely), and in particular Cadbury's Top-Deck ice-cream topped with vanilla custard. As told in the previous chapter, the next eight months in this stay-at-home, switched-off, meaningless zombie half-life was seen as a good result by those around me, including the psychiatrist - rather than the build-up to my next suicide attempt that it actually was.

This deceptive coercion to take Zyprexa needs to be contrasted with the truly genuine informed consent that I gave when I went on the Methadone. My Methadone doctor was honest with me and gave me plenty of information about Methadone and the program that went with it. He answered all my questions carefully and thoughtfully, and was frank with me about the experimental nature of my going on it. Methadone did not work for me either, but I hold no grudges towards my Methadone doctor about that. Maybe the Zyprexa was worth a try as an experiment too, like the Methadone. But the fundamental legal obligation of genuine informed consent was not honoured. On the contrary, I was manipulated and deceived.

To be fair to this psychiatrist, I should note that it was quite clear, and agreed to by me, that his role in my overall therapy program was never as an ongoing therapist or counsellor for my mental health issues. That is, the focus was still on my addiction problems, and these medications were really secondary to, and supportive of, the primary goal of getting off the heroin. In discussing the psycho-drugs he prescribed for me (Efexor and Zyprexa), he quite liked the metaphor I came up with that they were like the plaster cast you put over a broken bone to create a space in which the bone can heal. He never said anything as stupid as suggesting that these drugs fixed a chemical imbalance in my brain, as some psychiatrists do. He also knew that I was seeing Nicky for counselling, which he approved of and encouraged.

But I was not seeing Nicky very often by this time because I simply couldn't afford it. She had already been incredibly generous in adjusting her rates to accommodate me. I was on the pension by now, having blown almost all my accumulated wealth, mostly on heroin but also on seeking treatment and just living. Nicky was still of the view, and I didn't disagree, that I might benefit from some counselling with someone more skilled in crisis intervention and addiction than she was. Psychologists such as Phil were no longer an option as they could not be claimed on Medicare and I had already cancelled my private health insurance some time before. I had to look for a psychiatrist as the only affordable option, and Nicky gave me the name of one she did not know personally but about whom she had heard good things.

I saw this guy just twice. At the second appointment he prodded into my history and pain, where he deftly stirred up the deep well of sadness in me. I started crying, he kept prodding, and it became a gasping sob. This was difficult for me because, like many blokes, crying in front of others does not come easily, and is particularly uncomfortable when it becomes an uncontrollable, gagging sob. But I deliberately chose not to suppress it in this situation and allowed the tears to flow, wanting to believe that this emotional release was appropriate and even necessary for the 'therapy'. Then, quite suddenly, he looked at his watch, said 'OK, time's up', and got to his feet and left the room.

When he returned with his card swipe device for me to pay for the session I was still sobbing pretty uncontrollably. He looked at me and asked if I was angry with him. I was more preoccupied with my sobbing, so I was rather surprised by this question. But it made me think that, yes, I was angry with him, and I said so. I swear I saw a glint in his eye that said he was pleased with this. As I went to leave, still sobbing, I saw my anger more clearly and turned back to him and said that I was not angry with him that he had brought on my tears. Rather, I was angry that he could provoke such tears and then finish the session so abruptly simply because time was up. He just smiled at me, said nothing and I walked out. As I drove away, I realised that it was too dangerous to be driving sobbing like this and pulled over until I calmed down sufficiently.

This psychiatrist had also told me during that session that he was retiring in a month (he didn't mention this in my first session with him the week before). He said he could see me once more, maybe twice, before then if I wanted. I do not understand psychiatrists.

My living situation was pretty chaotic during this period and I was hoping to move in with my sister. But this didn't work out, largely because of her understandable concerns about my drug use, so I thought about retreating to the ashram again. I headed off in that direction but delayed and spent a night in a country pub. I was back on the heroin (again) and the return of this whole horrible, all-too-familiar, pattern seemed pointless and I couldn't face fronting up to the ashram. Besides, an ashram is not a place to detox and I knew that. I returned to Melbourne with, yet again, the intention of killing myself.

I checked into a motel in Footscray and once more got myself a lethal dose of heroin and also a bottle of whisky to add to all my psycho-drugs. After nearly three years, this was to be the first properly planned and serious attempt that I went ahead with. I woke up in hospital a day or so later. I have no memory of what happened, but apparently the motel staff let themselves into my room the next morning after the check-out time, saw me and called an ambulance. At the hospital my stomach was pumped with that awful charcoal stuff and other resuscitation measures were taken. Apparently there was a period when they were not sure whether I would come around or not and the doctors who revived me seemed almost as surprised as I was when I came to. They were not, however, as disappointed and furious about it as I was.

How awful for my family, who had been dreading for some years now that this day might eventually come. I heard later that most of them, as well as some of my friends, had had times when the phone rang and the caller started with something like 'I'm calling about David'. And they had all had the instant reaction of 'Is this it? Is he dead?' My poor family and friends. The doctors also told my family (but not me) that they had some concern about possible brain damage from this suicide attempt. Not because of the heroin but because of the psycho-drugs I had also taken.

It was a horrible few days after I woke up. One doctor wanted me to promise her that I wouldn't do it again - the so-called 'suicide contract'. How absurd! I said to her that if I couldn't make that promise to my dear brother sitting beside my bed in tears, how the hell did she think I could make such a promise to her? Then, when I was back on my feet and being transferred to another ward I did a runner to get some heroin on the streets of nearby Footscray.

My poor suffering brother came looking for me and begged me to come back to the hospital, but I refused to go until I scored. I needed a hit ... more than I needed air. Mike reluctantly conceded this knowing that he could not make me go back and that, maybe, just maybe, I would go back to the hospital if I had the hit that I was demanding. He had no choice really. I went and scored my hit and, as agreed, went back to Mike and returned to the hospital with him. Needless to say, this caused no end of mayhem back at the hospital, where they initially refused to readmit me. I was out of it and didn't care. But my family did, and they managed to persuade the doctors to readmit me - with the plausible argument that I would likely be dead soon if they didn't.

It was after this, my first serious attempt (since 1979, that is), that I finally went on the Methadone. My uncertain living situation was solved by a friend who invited me to join her in house-sitting the home of some friends of hers while they went overseas. I settled into the Methadone routine, on top of the anti-depressant and the stinking Zyprexa, with Cadbury's Top-Deck ice-cream (with vanilla custard) and daytime TV for company ... and became a placid, flaccid, zombie blob.

My next (and my last) serious suicide attempt came about six months later, when we had to move out of this house in early 1999. Although I had been seemingly 'stable' during this time - i.e. not actively suicidal nor using heroin - it was a far from satisfactory way of being. And although I was in a thick fog from all the prescription drugs, deep down I still felt that this was not a life worth living. When the time came that I had to look again for somewhere to live, I had neither the strength nor the wits to do anything constructive about it. I just plodded along, as I had for the last six months or so, into this waiting disaster.

All the while, everyone around me was reasonably content that I was apparently on the mend. I don't think I shared my private feelings about just how awful living this way was, largely because I was so unaware of it myself. I was just numb. But also, I was not seeing anyone for any regular counselling because I couldn't afford Nicky and was only making half-hearted attempts to find another psychiatrist. Like those around me, I also accepted this passive, meaningless life with some contentment. I should or could have realised that trouble was brewing, because I started stashing a portion of my take-away doses of the Methadone. I don't recall deliberately doing this as some long-term suicide plan - I just started doing it, and had secretly accumulated about fifteen doses. This is a poor description or explanation of what was going on within me, I know, but it really was a blur at the time and my recollection today is also blurred. With hindsight, I was clearly accumulating a lethal dose of Methadone, though not consciously aware at the time that this was what I was doing.

The previous chapter told the story of this attempt to OD with Methadone - waking up to the motel staff banging on the door, then driving around in a daze for a while before phoning the drug and alcohol clinic who called me in for a check-up. We pick up that story here with the same psychiatrist who had deceived me into taking the Zyprexa some six months previously. I still naively thought he was a reasonable guy and a good doctor. Hah! After a few preliminary questions he asked me where I would be staying that night. I said I didn't know. He asked me whether I would have another go at myself if he let me go. I said I didn't know. We circled round a few other questions, most of which I answered 'don't know', but he kept coming back to these two. My answers remained the same - it was the simple truth, I didn't have a clue. Finally, exasperated, he stood up and almost shouted at me, 'Do you know what your problem is, David?' I shrugged and he said, 'You just don't want to take responsibility for yourself!' I was stunned. I didn't say it to him at the time (though I wish I had) but I could only think that 'well, umm, yes doc, I did try to kill myself last night'.

He was left with no choice. He had to certify me. He tried to get me to change my mind ... or rather, to answer his questions, yet again, in the way that he wanted so that I could just leave. But my honest answer was still 'I don't know'. Besides, the psych hospital was as good a 'motel' as any other, as far as I was concerned. I didn't know and I didn't care. So after all the necessary paperwork, which I think infuriated this guy as it was getting late on a Friday afternoon, I found myself being escorted to Royal Park psychiatric hospital. Again, after nearly 20 years.

It was a very different place compared with 1979. First of all I was not in a lockup ward this time, even though I was an involuntary patient. There was a bit of a hassle organising the Methadone for me but otherwise it was a pretty quiet, laid back weekend as I waited to be assessed by the hospital psychiatrist on the Monday morning. I have since learned that the Mental Health Act requires that all involuntary psych patients must be assessed within twenty-four hours of admission. Having been admitted late on a Friday but not assessed until the Monday morning, I find the concept of 'next business day' an odd one for an involuntary psych ward.

This was to be my penultimate, and briefest, encounter with a psychiatrist. The 'assessment' was quite straightforward. After about a fifteen-minute consultation, he pronounced that my condition was an 'existential depression' and that I didn't need to be in the hospital. I was to be discharged immediately. They asked if I had somewhere to go and when I said no, I was given the phone number of the Salvation Army emergency accommodation. And then pretty much told to get on my bike. Have I mentioned that I don't understand psychiatrists? Despite a serious suicide attempt the previous Thursday, and with my history, this psychiatrist made a 'diagnosis' of 'existential depression' after knowing me for no more than fifteen minutes, and stated that I did not need whatever 'his' psychiatric hospital provided. I'm afraid I just don't get it.

I spent the next few nights staying with friends or family as we desperately looked for somewhere I could live. As my great good fortune would have it, I found a room in a rooming house in Fitzroy, which became my home for the next four years. Later I will be discussing at length the spiritual self-enquiry that was so critical to my recovery; but the significance of this safe, clean, affordable public housing cannot be overstated as an important contributory factor to my recovery, and indeed my survival. It was a tiny space and some of my fellow residents might not have been your first choice as neighbours. But it was home for four years, and this sense of 'home', no matter how meagre the home might be, is very important, possibly essential, if you are ever to find your 'self'.

We're getting close now to that magic time in June 1999 when freedom finally came. But before then I was to have one last 'therapeutic relationship' with a psychiatrist. This was also to be my last ever, because after this guy I promised myself that I would never again put myself in the hands of a psychiatrist. This may sound harsh, and is probably unfair to many good psychiatrists who presumably exist 'out there'. But this fellow was the sixth, and after finding a snake in the grass six out of six times, I'm no longer prepared to enter that territory again.

I had made attempts to see this very highly regarded psychiatrist before, but he was so solidly booked out that it had been impossible. When I moved into the rooming house after being discharged from Royal Park, I saw Nicky once or twice, and she was still encouraging me to find some professional help that I could afford. We pulled all the strings we could to see this guy, including my dad phoning him and, virtually in tears (or so the psychiatrist told me later), pleading with him to help his son. Eventually I had an appointment. By this time I had also decided that I was going to get off all the crazy psycho-drugs, and had started the slow process of weaning myself off the Methadone.

The ten or so sessions I had with this fellow are a difficult story to tell. It was not until several months after I had stopped seeing him that I finally came to see what was happening behind his closed doors. For the first few sessions he brought up - and kept coming back to - his notion of my 'foxiness', and how my efforts to get better were always a 'two-edged sword'. For instance, on the one hand I would reach out for help but then, rather than allow myself to be rescued, I would prefer to pull my rescuer into the whirlpool with me, or so he perceived it. Another observation he made, and the only one that I found useful, was that I had something of an addictive relationship to my suicidality - a suicide junkie, if you like. This was useful, as it highlighted how suicide had always been for me the final 'back door' through which I could escape. And yes, I needed that back door - I was dependent on it.

The main feature of these sessions was that, from the outset, anything I said was twisted and turned around and used against me. He always found some sinister, dark interpretation of anything I said, which he then threw back at me with his double-edged sword theory. When I eventually challenged him about this, saying that I was beginning to feel that I couldn't say anything without him twisting what I said in ways that were contrary both to my words and to their intended meaning, he then twisted this into 'evidence' of my foxiness. I felt as if he was always trying to beat me over the head with my own words. At times it was almost like some intellectual jousting game. In the end I figured that he must have seen me as some wild brumby that had to be tamed or 'broken' before any meaningful therapy could begin. But we never got that far. Thank heavens. Because after ten or so weeks of my thoughts and feelings constantly being denied by him, no real relationship had developed, so I got out of there. Thank heavens.

There were other problems too. Early on I had asked him whether I could talk with him about any suicidal *intentions* that I might be contemplating or planning. This was relevant because in the early days with him this was happening again. It was during this time that I had my last hit of heroin - hopefully forever - as I tried to soften the Methadone withdrawals. But I was also thinking a lot about suicide and twice went to a high place and tried to throw myself off, but couldn't do it. Like the last heroin hit, these have turned out to be my last two suicidal gestures - also hopefully forever.

I wanted to know, first of all, whether he would lock me up if I shared these private thoughts with him. I also wanted to find out whether this was something that I could talk with him about. It was in my thoughts and I felt it appropriate, perhaps necessary, for me to talk about it with him - or did I have to keep it secret, as is so often required? I had to find out whether this topic was allowed on the agenda at all. His response was clear. He simply didn't answer my question. Instead, this was one of the early instances for him of my foxiness, a game he seemed to think I was playing with him.

It was actually during the time with this psychiatrist that my blessed freedom arrived (a story to be told in later chapters). I didn't know for sure myself and inevitably had suspicions that it was just another fleeting 'high'. I tried to discuss this with him and described it as feeling on top of a wave. I had to decide whether to ride this wave, which might crash me onto the rocks, whether to trust it and go wherever it took me. To him this was just more foxiness. I guess it was understandable that he was not optimistic about the wave - who would be, with my history of 'relapses'? But what was not understandable was that he claimed the credit for this 'high' and its potential hope. I was stunned. On the one hand, he was dismissive of it, but then claimed the credit for it. Who was being 'foxy' this time? After only three or four sessions with him, and without any meaningful relationship yet, he wanted to claim that this was his doing! Not only did I think it ridiculous, I felt it was insulting to all those (including myself) who had struggled on my behalf for four long and painful years.

He also let slip in one conversation that he saw himself as my 'saviour'. One of my general 'rules-of-thumb' with therapy is not to trust those who would be your saviour. Sure, some people can help, and even play a critical role in the recovery process at times, but all the better therapists I know reject, as I do, the notion of 'therapist as saviour' as a dangerous attitude. So I was surprised to hear him say this and queried it, asking him, 'Did you just refer to yourself as my saviour?' He got quite sharp with me, waved his hand and dismissed my query with the retort, 'Don't play word games'. I let it drop, but felt this was a bit rich from a guy who was playing such word games with me.

The final falling out between us occurred when I wanted to leave town for a few weeks to visit friends in NSW. For me it was just a holiday, but for this psychiatrist it was a demonstration of my lack of commitment to therapy. We 'negotiated' quite hard on this and he was clearly trying to make a strong point. But I couldn't see it.

By this time, I was beginning to have some doubts about him but I didn't want just to throw in the towel and run away. If I were to leave, I wanted to make sure that I'd thought it through carefully and was sure it was for the right reasons. I talked it over with Nicky and my GP (who had written the referral for me to see this psychiatrist), two people that I did have meaningful therapeutic relationships with and who knew me pretty well. Both felt that if no real connection, communication or trust had been made after ten sessions then it probably wasn't working; nor was it likely to after this time. My GP did raise the relevant question of whether my 'quitting' was running away from therapy, and if so whether I needed to look at that as an issue. He concluded though, as I did too, that from his own experience with me he knew this was not an issue, so he figured that I just wasn't 'clicking' with this particular psychiatrist.

I decided to stop seeing the psychiatrist. I called and left a message on his answering service. Over the next day or so I found that I felt a huge relief that I would not be seeing this man any more, and I knew that I had made the right decision. I was still riding that wave of peace and freedom that had arrived and was becoming more and more confident that it wasn't taking me onto the rocks. But even so, I was surprised at the relief I felt from ending the battles I had been having with this guy.

He called me back a couple of days later and recommended that I continue seeing him. He urged me to see him at least once more to talk through my decision to stop therapy. I told him I would think about it and call him back. It was with some bemusement (and amusement) that I pondered how he had never believed anything I told him. Why would I want to waste my time and money to tell him my reasons for ending therapy with him, which he presumably wouldn't believe either? I called the next day and left a message that I could not think of any reason why I might want to see him again, and if he really wanted to learn why I was 'quitting' then he could contact my GP (whom he might believe).

This should have been the end of it, and I would have simply proceeded with the delightful new peace and freedom that was really starting to flood through my life. But some months later I went to see my GP (about something else) and he told me that he had received a letter from the psychiatrist about me. It was supposedly one of those 'right and proper' professional letters that is sent to the referring doctor at times like this. I was curious, of course, and quizzed my GP about it. As he pulled it out of his file he casually remarked that his recollection was that the letter said mostly nice things about me. I was a bit surprised by this and asked to see it. My GP hesitated and said that he needed to read it again to check first. I said no, now that he had revealed that this letter existed, I wanted a copy of it. He chuckled at my assertiveness and agreed to hand it over, though he still read it again, just to check. He still felt that it mostly said nice things about me.

But that was not how I read it. What I saw on my first reading of this letter was that first and foremost it was a 'cover your ass' letter. The psychiatrist was getting on the record his interpretation of our time together. At one level this is quite appropriate and probably very sensible. If I did happen to suicide shortly after my time with him, then such a record written prior to the suicide would be useful protection for him and I don't see anything wrong with that, as long as the truth is being told that is. I pointed out to my GP that this reputation protection and ass-saving was what the letter was really about, and that it was not some courteous 'for your information' letter as it pretended to be. There were some glaring factual errors, but of more concern were the subtle but quite sinister misrepresentations that presented a very distorted version of our time together.

I read this letter carefully several times over the following days, and became more and more outraged when I saw what this man was doing. I felt obliged to write a response to it, which I asked my GP to keep in his files as a correction to the one he held from the psychiatrist. I'm actually very grateful for this letter for several reasons. First, it confirmed for me my worst fears about the psychiatrist, so that I felt another surge of relief that I was free of him. Second, it gave me a valuable insight into the inner workings of his psychiatric double-speak and the prejudices with which he had bullied me. And finally, this letter prompted me to write a reply. Although I had always enjoyed writing, I had not written at all for at least a couple of years. My suicidality had frozen my writing hand, and I had abandoned writing as just another pointless exercise. So I had to resurrect my writing skills to craft a careful response to this shocking letter. I've been writing regularly ever since, and, with some irony, I'm grateful to the psychiatrist for this unintended therapeutic contribution to my life today.

In the interest of brevity, and also because I do not want to personalise my criticisms of psychiatry, I will only mention a few of the key points arising from this correspondence. The most obvious flaws in his letter were some simple factual errors. He referred to hangups I had about my 'working-class family', noting to my GP that 'his personal and family history is probably well known to you so I won't go into it'. Well, yes, my GP was familiar with my family background so at least he knew that it was not at all working-class. My father was a pretty successful businessman, I went to a posh private school and we grew up in Camberwell - it doesn't get much more middle-class than that. The psychiatrist couldn't tell my GP any of this in his letter, for the simple reason that, after more than ten hours with me, he had simply not enquired about my family background at all. This is odd enough by itself, but then to invent a fictitious working-class family for me is decidedly peculiar. There must have been a reason. I have no doubt that this invention revealed the prejudices of the psychiatrist. And I suspect that he saw me as not of his own 'class'.

More sinister than these simple factual errors, but no less prejudiced, was his 'diagnosis' of my 'disorder'. He mentions, in this letter to my GP, 'sado-masochism' and 'personality disorder', though he admits that he didn't use this language with me (which is true) because 'he doesn't find such language helpful'. I was alarmed to see myself being described as sado-masochistic, but was reassured by Nicky and my GP that the clinical meaning of this is very different to the Marquis de Sade fetishism that is commonly understood by this term. I thought long and hard about this, wanting to understand what this man was seeing in me that he chose to describe in this way. I talked with Nicky and my GP about it and in the end concluded, with them, that what he seemed to be seeing, and using this language to describe, was my passion and intensity. Nicky and my GP, along with my family and good friends, are familiar with this passionately intense side of my personality and also that this can be an aspect of my self-destructive behaviour when it emerges.

Back in 1999 I had no idea what 'personality disorder' meant. I have since learned that he was probably diagnosing me with 'borderline' personality disorder, which is one of the most disreputable and insidious of the diagnostic categories of modern psychiatry. But at the time of this letter, my main concern about these 'diagnoses' was how he kept them to himself.

When I saw his words to my GP I recognised in his 'sado-masochism' the 'foxiness' and 'two-edged sword' that were so central to my time with him. Somehow he thought that these metaphors were more useful than a formal diagnosis, even though I had asked him explicitly what he thought was wrong with me. I find this very sneaky, and again wonder why he felt he had to play these games with me. Isn't it negligent and unprofessional and unethical conduct for a doctor to deliberately withhold his or her diagnosis from a patient? Withholding a diagnosis disempowers us. Without this information I am unable to do my own research into my so-called illness, including getting a second opinion. It is manipulative, shows a gross disrespect for the patient, and is an abuse of the therapeutic relationship. I have subsequently learned that these diagnostic categories of psychiatry are highly speculative and regularly used in this manipulative, disrespectful and abusive way. These days, with hindsight, I'm not very surprised that he shared them with his fellow medico but not with me.

I could not let this misrepresentation of my time with this

psychiatrist go unchallenged as the 'official record' of our time together, so I wrote a response to it. This response was addressed to my GP, firstly because the original letter was to him, but also because I knew that my words were wasted on the psychiatrist. I asked my GP to file my response alongside the original letter and gave him permission to forward it to the psychiatrist if he wanted to. I don't know if he ever did this though, and I've never heard from that psychiatrist again.

It was this psychiatrist, even more than the one who deceived me into taking the Zyprexa, who finally put the fear of psychiatry into me forever. It's easy to be critical of psychiatrists who deceive you into taking dangerous, potent psycho-drugs. And rightly so. But it was actually my experience with this last psychiatrist, the sixth and worst of six bad experiences with psychiatry, which prompted my promise to myself to never put myself in the hands of a psychiatrist again. Although perhaps not so blatantly abusive as forced or coercive drug 'therapies', it is the arrogant prejudices and deceitful manipulations that I encountered with this man that most frighten me. I was now able to see these prejudices and deceptions in all the relationships that I'd had with psychiatrists. And I have since learned that this is not just a few 'rotten apples' in the psychiatric barrel but is endemic and intrinsic to the modern practice of psychiatry - that is, such prejudices and deceptions are the very foundation of the profession.

*   *   *   *   *

Following my recovery, I still had a need to make sense of all that I'd been through, so I went to a library and looked up 'suicide' in the catalogue. This was to be my introduction to suicidology, and what I found startled me sufficiently to lead me to study it further, culminating in the PhD that I completed in 2006.

My first reaction to the literature of suicidology was that I found myself feeling uneasy about the common taxonomy used to distinguish between suicide contemplators, attempters and completers.[1] I then saw that my discomfort was that I didn't recognise my story in any of these categories. It was as if these were three different types of people, and I was none of them. Although I was looking for any mention of spirituality, I guess I was not too surprised to find nothing at all on this. I was, however, surprised to find so little of what I now call the first-person voice of living with suicidal feelings. The actual suicidal person was barely perceptible in this learned, expert literature, which made me feel that these experts were looking at people like me through the wrong end of their telescope.

Suicide is usually viewed as a mental health issue, which locates it within the wider mental health industry. This partly explains some of the gaps in the thinking about suicide that we find in suicidology, but there are also some distinct differences from mainstream mental health. First, suicidology is rather better than mainstream mental health (though still not great) at taking the social context of the suicidal person into consideration. On the other hand, it is very much worse than mainstream mental health at including the first-person or 'consumer' perspective of the suicidal person – this may alarm some mental health consumer advocates who might think it couldn't possibly be worse, but there is not even the tokenistic participation that they are familiar with. Perhaps the biggest distinction (and saving grace in some ways) is that suicidality is not a psychiatric diagnosis – which places it slightly to one side of mainstream mental health.

To appreciate these distinctions and their significance, a short crash course on 'suicidology' will help. But first, a reality check is needed to remind us that in day-to-day life, if you disclose that you're having suicidal thoughts then you will very likely get a psychiatric diagnosis, which in turn will probably lead to psychiatric treatment, most likely drugs, and there is also a very real risk that you will be locked up and forced to take these drugs whether you consent or not. We look at this more closely later, but first a little suicidology.

These days suicidology is its own distinct academic and professional discipline though its origins can still be seen as coming from three 'parent disciplines' – sociology, psychology and psychiatry. One of the first scholarly studies of suicide was by the pioneering French sociologist Émile Durkheim back in the late nineteenth century, and his book *Le Suicide* is regarded as a classic in the literature of suicidology.

Although Durkheim's taxonomy of four different types of suicide is still of interest, his greatest legacy is the ubiquitous epidemiological study that still makes up the vast bulk of suicide research. A key aim of these studies is to try and identify 'risk factors' for suicide in order to predict specific groups of high risk people. They are important studies for targeting suicide prevention programs but, as always, statistical data such as this is unable to predict the suicide risk of any specific individual within a particular demographic group. It must also be said that, although these studies give us much important information, they have also been rather disappointing. Consistently, the highest risk factor for suicide reported from these studies is a previous suicide attempt, which I confess made me laugh when I first read it as it appears that killing yourself, like most other things in life, takes practice. It also bothers me that so much of the suicide research budgets around the world seem to be spent on ever more epidemiological studies.

I won't dwell any further on sociology, because when we're feeling suicidal and want help we don't go to the yellow pages and look up 'sociologist'. For interventions aimed at assisting a suicidal individual we will most likely turn to psychology or psychiatry. This raises a question that I still get asked occasionally, which is 'what is the difference between psychology and psychiatry?' This will be answered in the following discussion, but a more interesting question is why are there these two distinct 'psych' professions, and how do we choose which to turn to for help?

Psychology has influenced suicidology in many ways but I'll focus on one of the great pioneers of suicidology – indeed I believe he first coined this word back in the 1950s – Professor Edwin S. Shneidman. I had the great privilege of a brief meeting with Professor Shneidman when I visited the US in 2007, just a couple of years before his death in 2009, aged 91.

Shneidman is one of the notable exceptions among suicidologists in that he gives due recognition to the first-person voice of the suicidal person. As he describes it:

> the keys to understanding suicide are made of plain language … the proper language of suicidology is lingua franca – the ordinary everyday words that are found in the verbatim reports of beleaguered suicidal minds

As a psychologist, Shneidman attributes suicide to psychological pain due to frustrated, thwarted or distorted psychological needs, which he calls *psychache*. As with physical pain in medicine, psychache obliges the suicidologist to look deeper for the source of the pain, which Shneidman does by seeking the unfulfilled psychological needs that a suicidal person might be struggling with. Before he died, I tried on a couple of occasions to persuade Professor Shneidman to amend his definition of psychache to include spiritual needs as well as psychological ones. I was not successful, but he was not disdainful of my suggestion, as most other suicidologists are. On the contrary, his response to my talk of spirituality likened it to the need for an adequate phenomenology of suicide, which he agreed was desperately lacking from suicidology. I laughed and said I'd settle for this as a first step towards bringing spiritual needs into our collective thinking about suicide.

Shneidman was worried that his ideas on suicide might be lost after he died. Fortunately there are some suicidologists who recognise the importance of the concept of psychache and are now the torch-bearers of his great legacy. In particular, there is a small group of suicidologists known as the Aeschi Group, who are the other notable exception within mainstream suicidology in taking seriously the first-person voice of the suicidal person. Taking their name from the Swiss town where they held their first few conferences, the Aeschi Group put the suicidal person at the centre of the therapeutic process. In particular, they emphasise that it is suicidal people's lived experience *in their own words* that is the 'gold standard' for understanding a suicidal crisis, and the starting point for any therapeutic intervention.

Shneidman and the Aeschi Group are critical of the trend in recent decades towards the increasing medicalisation of suicide. The third parent discipline of suicidology, psychiatry, is responsible for this trend, as it is the dominant influence in the field these days. Whereas psychology sees the mind in familiar human terms of thoughts and feelings – intentions, desires, love and grief, joy and sadness, and so on – modern psychiatry sees the mind largely in terms of the biology of the brain. And unlike psychology, psychiatry is primarily concerned with pathology – illness, disorder, disease and, yes, 'abnormality'. The decline of psychology's influence on suicidology during Professor Shneidman's later years corresponds with the rise of biological psychiatry, or *biopsychiatry*, throughout the wider mental health field.

As a branch of medicine, the two key elements of psychiatry are its diagnostic system and the treatments it prescribes. For diagnosis, the *Diagnostic and Statistical Manual of Mental Disorders*, or *DSM*, is the 'Bible' of modern psychiatry. And the primary mode of treatment for psychiatric disorders is psychoactive medications. Both are controversial. To illustrate the typical practice of modern psychiatry, including the controversies, we will look at depression as the most common psychiatric diagnosis associated with suicide.

The *DSM* avoids any causal – or etiological – explanations for the nearly 300 disorders that it catalogues. Rather, psychiatric disorders are defined solely in terms of symptoms that are statistically analysed according to how they cluster together. Once a distinct cluster has been identified it is then declared to be a psychiatric disorder by the DSM committee of psychiatrists. The assumption here is that a cluster of symptoms corresponds to an underlying disorder which, these days, biopsychiatry then assumes to be a biological, medical illness. And the myth of mental illness is born. These are rather grand (or grandiose) assumptions that are hotly contested by many experts around the world, including quite a few dissenting psychiatrists. We do not see anything like this degree of controversy about the diagnostic methods used by other branches of medicine.

The *DSM* defines Major Depressive Disorder using nine symptoms. For a diagnosis, it says that at least five of these symptoms must be present for at least two weeks. A few qualifications are made, such as that at least one of two specific symptoms must be present, and some exemptions are made if the symptoms can be attributed to, for instance, physical illness, the effects of drugs or 'normal' bereavement. A further requirement is that the symptoms must cause 'clinically significant' distress or functional impairment.

If you look at the list of symptoms, they are all common, everyday difficulties that we all experience from time to time, with the possible exception of the ninth symptom, suicidal ideation. The others are sadness, problems with sleeping or appetite, fatigue, poor concentration and so on. Even if you take into account a severity measure for each symptom, there are still lots of possible explanations for why a person may exhibit these symptoms. The clearest illustration of this is that depression defined this way is indistinguishable from sleep deprivation. But modern psychiatry regards these criteria as sufficient to 'declare' this cluster of symptoms as a psychiatric disorder – the mental illness of depression.

Professor Shneidman criticises the *DSM*'s scientific validity as 'too much specious accuracy built on a false epistemology'. The specious accuracy he refers to is the statistical analysis – meaningless because it is based on the false epistemology of assuming that the simple clustering of symptoms corresponds to an underlying disorder, illness or disease. Imagine if other branches of medicine applied this diagnostic method.

The next big leap of faith of biopsychiatry is that it then assumes that psychiatric disorders are due to a biological malfunction of the brain. This has given rise to the 'chemical imbalance of the brain' theory of psychiatric disorders, sometimes called the 'broken brain' school of psychiatry. With depression, the chemical that we hear about most is the neurotransmitter serotonin which has acquired the status of 'mood chemical of the brain'. But there is actually no solid scientific evidence for this.

What we do know about serotonin is that it plays a role in the regulation of sleep, appetite and libido, amongst other things. We also know that it seems to act as a brake on impulsive urges, so its lack may indeed play a role in suicide, though it is also a gross exaggeration to call it the suicide chemical of the brain. Another feature of serotonin that is rarely mentioned is that most of the serotonin in the body is not in the brain at all. And serotonin is just one of hundreds of neurotransmitters, most of which we know even less about than we do about serotonin. The final and most damning weakness of the serotonin theory of depression is that biopsychiatry has no pathology test for depression. It cannot even give me a measure of what a healthy serotonin level might be for a middle-aged male like me, far less the variations that might exist across age and gender, etc. Despite the great advances made in brain science in recent years, the current reality is that what we do know about the biology of the brain is still very much less than what we don't yet know.

The exaggerated claims of biopsychiatry, along with its reductionist biological determinism, are why the metaphor of 'mental illness' is now running amok as a literal truth. As a metaphor the phrase may have some merit (though not much in my view), but the mind is not the brain. The mind is not a biological organ that can get ill or diseased in the way that the brain can. Mental distress cannot be fully understood solely in terms of the biology of the brain. Psychology knows this, but the biological fundamentalism of modern psychiatry denies it. Professor Shneidman's psychache concept helps us see that calling so-called depression a mental *illness* makes about as much sense as calling physical pain a disease.

The best that can be said about the scientific status of psychiatry's current diagnostic system is that it has some scientific validity as a hypothesis. It is, however, looking like a rather weak hypothesis, given the billions of dollars that have already been spent trying to validate it without any success. In the psychiatric literature you will find psychiatrists discussing among themselves the lack of validity and reliability of its diagnostic system, though they try to counter this with the questionable assertion that this does not matter too much so long as it has utility. It is clear that the real power behind the myth of mental illness is not any good scientific evidence but rather the social and political power of the profession of psychiatry.

The mental illness metaphor really starts to run amok when we look at the treatment side of modern psychiatry. If depression is *assumed* to be a medical illness caused by a biological malfunction of the brain, in this case low serotonin levels, then biopsychiatry *assumes* that the remedy is to 'fix' this biological malfunction, primarily through psychoactive drugs. For depression, these days, this usually means anti-depressants that supposedly boost a person's serotonin levels.

There is now a vast and growing literature on the shortcomings of most psychiatric medications, in terms both of their efficacy and their safety. The efficacy of the most popular anti-depressants, for instance, is increasingly being shown to be largely due to the placebo effect. And their negative side-effects have become a major concern. These include the very real risk of addiction problems, despite psychiatry's persistent denial that these drugs are addictive. Of even greater concern, these drugs have been shown actually to induce suicidal thoughts and behaviour in some people, so much so that some countries require a specific warning about this in the packaging on these drugs.

My own view is that these drugs can help some people sometimes, but that they need to be used with great caution. I base this view on people I know who report that the drugs do help them, even though that was not my own experience of them. But I've not met anyone who says that the drugs have 'fixed' their depression, only that they have helped them to 'manage' it. We can take our cue again from Professor Shneidman's psychache concept to see that these drugs are best understood as psychological painkillers. In this way they can be compared to morphine, which is certainly worth taking when you break a leg, but will not mend the broken bone. As psychological painkillers, these drugs can sometimes ease the pain and buy you some time to address the real issues, the real source of your pain. But to be told that you need to take these drugs for the rest of your life because you have a chemical balance of the brain is really a wicked deception.

The running amok of the mental illness myth gets even worse if, like me, you don't respond to the anti-depressants. When this happens, the bio-fundamentalists bring out their big guns, in my case the anti-psychotic drug Zyprexa. These drugs are supposed to be for the treatment of the so-called psychotic disorders but in recent years there has been a massive increase in their use for other diagnoses. Because of 'off-label' prescribing – i.e. for disorders other than what it's been approved for – Zyprexa in particular has become a bonanza drug for its manufacturer, Eli Lilly. One of the primary off-label uses of Zyprexa is for what's called 'treatment resistant' depression – as in my story – which is really just an admission by psychiatry that it has run out of ideas – as in my story.

The running amok becomes extreme when the flimsy, speculative science of psychiatry, for both diagnosis and treatment, then becomes the rationale for imposing these treatments on people without their consent. As noted previously, the serious human rights issues here are beyond the scope of this book, so I'll just repeat that psychiatric force – or more accurately, psychiatric assault – can contribute to nudging an already distressed, fragile and vulnerable person over the edge into suicide.

The combined myths that depression is a medical illness and that it is the major cause of suicide do not stand up to scrutiny. You might occasionally hear advocates of these myths claim that anti-depressants are reducing the suicide toll. This is myth-making at work. When you examine the fine print of the studies making this claim, you will see that the evidence is very thin. First of all, where there have been reductions in the suicide toll they have tended to be with very specific sub-groups, such as with aged people or, as we have recently seen in Australia, with young, rural males. This begs the question, why have anti-depressants not reduced the suicide toll more uniformly throughout the community, given the massive and widespread increases in their consumption over the last few decades? The likely answer to this is that it is probably other interventions, not anti-depressants, that are responsible for the occasional, selective drops in the suicide numbers. More generally, what we have seen is suicide rates continuing to climb, or at least not fall significantly, in many parts of the world where this massive consumption of anti-depressants is happening. The real question that needs to be asked is why this mass consumption of anti-depressants has failed to reduce the suicide toll.

The profession of psychiatry has been compared to the emperor with no clothes. I'm all for good neuroscience helping us to understand the biology of the brain, which I'm sure can also contribute to our understanding of the psychology of the mind. But neuroscience will never replace psychology. We need to understand the mind as well as the brain – the psychology of the mind cannot be reduced to the biology of the brain. Psychiatrists, it seems to me, try to be both neuroscientist and psychologist but unfortunately end up being not very good at either.

Many suicidologists would claim that their philosophy these days is what's called the *biopsychosocial* approach, representing the merger of the three parent disciplines. Indeed, many mental health practitioners regard the biopsychosocial approach as the state of the art for mental health practice more broadly. I would not disagree and we will have a brief look at this soon. But it must be emphasised that biopsychiatry now dominates the mental health industry in general and, through this, contaminates suicidology. Perhaps the most revealing admission of this reality comes from no lesser person than a former president of the American Psychiatric Association, Dr Steven Sharfstein, who in 2008 lamented how his profession had 'allowed the biopsychosocial model to become the bio-bio-bio model'.

We have already seen the psychosocial approach in the drug addiction chapter, where it is summarised as recovery-oriented, strengths-based, holistic, socially aware, participatory and non-coercive. This was contrasted with the medical model's deficit-based emphasis on the treatment of illness from a narrow biological perspective that expects passivity rather than participation from the patient and, in mental health, is often coercive. The biopsychosocial approach adds the biological knowledge of medicine to the psychosocial model to achieve a more holistic, whole-of-person, way of understanding and helping people experiencing psychosocial distress – whether it be drug addiction, madness or suicide. But medicine has to become just one of many equal partners within this approach. A cry you will hear from the psychosocial sector is 'doctors on tap, not on top'.

A further refinement of the state of the art in mental health that we are seeing these days is being called the 'trauma informed' approach. This fits neatly with Professor Shneidman's psychache concept in that it looks beyond just the symptomatic pain for some traumatic experiences in the history of someone experiencing psychosocial distress. Such trauma can take many forms, and there are now good studies showing that, in one form or another, it is found in the majority of people presenting with mental health symptoms. With such strong data indicating this, many are arguing that trauma assessment needs to become standard procedure, with recovery-based supports being provided as appropriate. This is already close to standard practice in many drug and alcohol services, plus a few other services such as some for refugees and asylum seekers, many of whom have experienced torture or great physical suffering, or witnessed atrocities. The challenge for mental health and suicide prevention is to overcome the biological fundamentalism of biopsychiatry and embrace a genuine biopsychosocial approach.

The World Health Organisation defines health as 'a state of complete physical, mental and social well-being, and not merely the absence of disease or infirmity', which is a biopsychosocial definition of health. Despite this, if you look at the WHO literature you will find that its own usage of this term is not always consistent with this definition. In many cases, if you look at the context, the usage and the meaning of the term 'health' in these documents is obviously referring to the narrower definition that can more precisely be called 'medical health'. To distinguish between these two quite different meanings, it is useful to adopt the word 'well-being' for the WHO's official definition of health – and leave 'health' for just medical health, which is how the WHO tends to use it anyway.

Well-being is also in some ways a better word than 'recovery', with its links to the term 'rehabilitation'. I know people who protest against these words, saying that they don't want to be 're-' anything. Although recovery for some people is about returning to some previous state of well-being, such as becoming free of your drug addictions or re-establishing broken relationships, this is not always the case. The notion of well-being is a rather better term than 'recovery' for accommodating all the ways that we might be able to 'live well', and a very much better one than 'health' with its implicit medical connotations.

A problem still remains though. My freedom from persistent suicidal despair, my well-being today, came about by moving into altogether new psychospiritual territory. It was neither medicine's biology of the body (brain) nor psychology's understanding of the mind that made this possible. Indeed, these forms of knowledge not only did not help but sometimes made my suicidal crisis of the self worse – especially psychiatry's aggressive biological fundamentalism that denies both mind and spirit.

Suicidology, Professor Shneidman's psychache concept, and the WHO definition of health, all need to be updated to take into account spiritual well-being as part of our overall well-being. Before resuming the story of how I found my freedom, we now take a brief interlude to look into contemporary thinking about our sense of self, another largely ignored concept in mental health, which in fact turned out to be my doorway to freedom.

Note

1. Suicidology also addresses the issue of deliberate self-harming behaviour that is not necessarily suicidal, sometimes called 'parasuicide'. The key issue here is the degree of suicidal intent. For some people, the suicidal intent is very clear, while at other times there is often some uncertainty, ambiguity or ambivalence. Some other people self-harm, even in quite risky and potentially lethal ways, with absolutely no suicidal intent – indeed they are often offended if this is imputed to them. Although this is an

inevitably blurred boundary, this book is not about the latter end of this spectrum of suicidal intent – the focus here is on understanding suicidal intentions.

INTERLUDE

Who Am I?

If there is one idea that I hope people might take from this book it is that *suicide is best understood as a crisis of the self.* There are several reasons why this is a more useful way of thinking about suicide than the current emphasis on it as a mental health issue. First, it is really a statement of the obvious, but one that has become lost in all the 'mental illness' noise. There is no concept more central to the study of suicide than that of the self, the 'sui' in suicide, both the victim and perpetrator of any suicidal act. Second, thinking about suicide as a crisis of the self corresponds more closely to the lived experience of suicidal feelings. To know suicidal distress 'from the inside' is to know it as a crisis of the self. And third, if we re-conceptualise our thinking about suicide as a crisis of the self, then it automatically raises some important questions that suicidology currently largely ignores, such as the question one brave suicidologist did dare to ask, 'Who or what is killing whom?'[1]

In this Interlude we take a brief pause in our thinking about suicide to look at some of the contemporary thinking about the self and subjectivity. We first revisit suicidology's three parent disciplines – psychiatry, psychology and sociology – to look at their current thinking about the self beyond just what they say about it as it relates to suicide (which is not much). This will lead to thinking about the nature of the self in what we might broadly call 'postmodern' philosophy, where the self and subjectivity have been lively topics for half a century or more.

To begin with the very simplest view of the self, modern biological psychiatry reduces us all to biochemical robots – selfless, soul-less, meaningless biochemical zombies (even before we take their drugs), whose subjective, lived experience is completely irrelevant. As a branch of medicine, biopsychiatry sees itself as a 'traditional' science where knowledge is based on scientific methods that rely on data that is objective, observable, measurable, testable, repeatable and so on. According to this notion of science, the only valid and reliable knowledge is so-called 'objective' knowledge, the common shorthand phrase for this kind of science.

With the elevation of objective knowledge as the only valid knowledge has come a corresponding invalidation or denial of the validity of subjective knowledge. Both these words, objective and subjective, have now become such loaded terms – basically objective is good, subjective is bad – that I prefer not to use them at all. I prefer to distinguish between the *third-person* knowledge for traditional so-called objective scientific knowledge, and the *first-person* knowledge of phenomena that can only be known through the subjective, lived experience of them.

The traditional third-person knowledge of medicine has demonstrated its excellence for understanding flesh and bone, disease and injury. I have the greatest respect for good third-person science. Indeed the burns I suffered back in 1979 might have been fatal if it had not been for the brilliant medical and surgical knowledge of my doctors. But third-person knowledge is limited when there is nothing for the third-person observer to observe. A good first example of this is pain, which is primarily something that is subjectively experienced rather than something that can be observed (the screams can be observed but this is not the pain that is experienced by the screamer). Medicine now actually appreciates this much better than it used to. These days, when a doctor wants to try and get a measure of someone's pain they typically ask their patient how severe their pain is on a scale of one to ten. The patient's answer is first-person data based on first-person experiential knowledge.

Another striking example of first-person knowledge is love. Love is only known through the felt experience of it. It cannot be observed in any 'objective' way – there is no 'love-ometer' that we can use to measure it. But most of us would recognise love as 'real', that love exists in the universe and, what's more, that it is something of significance. Love, like most first-person knowledge, is not discussed at suicidology conferences.

If we ignore or deny the first-person dimensions of our sense of self then we can end up with the concept of self that we find today in biological psychiatry, where we are all biochemical robots or, as Francis Crick so aptly put it, 'we are nothing but a pack of neurons'. This is largely what we find in suicidology today. A major current reference in suicidology is the *Comprehensive Textbook of Suicidology*, in which we find suicidology defined as 'the *science* of self-destructive behaviors'. It then asserts a very third-person kind of science when it says that 'surely any science worth its salt ought to be true to its name and be as objective as it can, make careful measurements, count something'.[2]

Turning to psychology, the second parent discipline of suicidology, we find that the self and subjectivity have been major themes throughout its history. A useful starting point is the American pioneer of psychology at the turn of the twentieth century, William James, whose approach to exploring the self is still characteristic of psychology today. James proposed a tripartite model of the self – the material self (one's body and possessions), the social self (the impressions one gives to others), and a spiritual self (one's inner, subjective being).

It is interesting that James recognised the spiritual dimension of our sense of self, which he explores in his famous lectures on *The Varieties of Religious Experience*. But the key feature of James's approach is his dissection of the self into several component parts. For over a hundred years, psychology has been dissecting the self into many different component parts, but without, as yet, reaching any general agreement on what all these various components are. For example, one psychological model of the self talks about the *individual, relational* and *collective* selves.[3] Another dissects the self into the self as *reflexive consciousness* (self-awareness), the self as *interpersonal being* (the social/relational self) and the self as *agent* or *executive function* (the ability to make choices, take action, exert control etc). On top of these and other taxonomies of the self, there seems to be an ever-growing list of properties of the self, such as self-knowledge, self-conceptions, self-presentation, self-regulation and the ubiquitous self-esteem, to mention just a few. The psychology of the self is a very busy domain of enquiry.[4]

Apart from the continuing lack of agreement about the various components of the self, the problem here is that in dissecting the self in this way the most important property of the lived experience of the self is often lost. The unified, continuous wholeness or sense of *identity* that we feel as a self as it is lived – as an individual person with a self – is lost by these taxonomies.

We need to revisit psychiatry at this point and look at the psychoanalytical school of psychiatry, which by the standards of modern biological psychiatry is best viewed as a psychological approach more concerned with the mind than the brain. Sigmund Freud, the founding father of psychoanalysis, distinguished between a conscious mind and an unconscious mind. This *divided self* has since permeated our thinking about the self, to become Freud's most enduring legacy. Freud's heir apparent, Carl Jung, introduced the idea of a *collective unconscious*, expanding the self beyond the boundaries of just an individual self and hinting at his interest in spirituality, which Freud regarded as a neurosis and was central to his very public falling out with Jung. Once more, the key ideas here are about dissecting the self into its component parts. And once again, there is no general agreement on these components, nor which component is responsible for the critical subjective sense of a unified, continuous self, or how they might work together to produce this.

These early days of psychology coincided with the decline in the influence of religion in western intellectual circles. At the turn of the twentieth century, Nietzsche made his famous declaration that 'God is dead'. Prior to this, religious beliefs were central to our sense of self, but now a new 'home' for the self had to be found. The new site for the self became the mind, and psychology as the science of the mind also became the science of the self. Psychology now faced a problem that has perplexed philosophers for centuries – the apparent *duality* of the self. In recent times Deborah Prentice has described this problem, with reference to William James, as:

> Perhaps the most enduring of all questions about the self concerns its dual nature: How can we conceive of an entity that is, at once, both a known object and the knower of that object? This question has compelled and confounded philosophers and psychologists for hundreds of years. Most have approached the problem by distinguishing the knower from the known, the I from the me, in James' terms, and theorising about the two components of the self separately.[5]

Once again the dual self is a divided self, this time between the 'I' who knows the self subjectively, and what James calls the 'me', or the self that can be known objectively. Until very recently, psychology has largely heeded the advice of the distinguished American psychologist Gordon Allport in the 1960s that 'psychologists should concern themselves only with the self as a known object and leave the self as knower to the philosophers'.

Before we turn to the philosophers though, we must look at suicidology's third parent discipline, sociology, where again we find the self divided. Some of the social aspects of our sense of self have already been mentioned above, such as concepts of the relational or social self. Indeed, social psychology is a distinct and significant sub-discipline within psychology. Many people see the self primarily in terms of our relationships with others, so that the social, relational self is the primary component in these models of many selves, while others give primacy to the individual self. I do not take a side in this argument, for I find the starting premise of a divided self as fundamentally flawed. A further weakness of the social or relational model of the self is that it sees the self in terms of relationship with some other self, which is a rather circular, even tautological, argument that doesn't seem to help us very much. Although dissecting the self into many parts has provided many useful insights, it has inevitably proved rather inadequate for understanding the most critical aspect of our subjective experience of the self as a whole unified, continuous identity.

Contemporary thinking about the self and subjectivity has played a key role in what is now typically called a 'postmodern' view of the world. Getting familiar with contemporary postmodern thinking, or just 'postmodernism', is a pretty daunting and often disheartening task. A useful starting point is to look at the modern era and what distinguishes it from the earlier pre-modern era and the postmodern era now upon us. For this, I am indebted to the American philosopher Ken Wilber who talks of the 'great dignity' and the 'great disaster' of modernity to highlight both the good and the bad of these transitions from the old to the new.

The modern era, sometimes called the Age of Enlightenment or the Age of Reason or just 'modernity', is marked by the rise of rational, scientific thinking. The divine right to rule of inherited power and the dogmatic authority of religion were challenged by the intellectual power of reason; of rational, scientific thinking and knowledge. With this came the great social advances of the era, such as democratic governments, the end of slavery, the emancipation of women, the separation of power between church and state, and so on. Although some of these projects are still unfinished, the rational principles behind them are now generally accepted. In what we now call mental health, the rise of modernity marked the shift from viewing madness as something supernatural, such as possession by the devil or the wages of sin, to it being viewed as a health issue. Along with all the other great social changes mentioned above, this does indeed represent the 'great dignity of modernity' compared to the pre-modern era it replaced.

The world was changed forever by this great dignity of modernity, a radical shift from pre-modern to modern ways of thinking. Using rational argument and systematic, empirical methods of enquiry, science challenged the dogmatic, ideological authority of church, dynasty and patriarchy. Along with their technological achievements, science and rational argument radically changed the social, cultural and political landscape.

But in the last half-century or so, another equally radical transition has commenced, where the science of modernity, which has served us so well in so many ways, has now been exposed as limited. Science had become exalted so that rational, objective ways of knowing acquired supremacy as at least the best, if not the only, path to truth, and the only kind of valid knowledge. Other ways of knowing – aesthetic, subjective, inter-subjective, moral, spiritual and others – were marginalised, their validity denied, so that they have been progressively excluded from scientific enquiry. The science of modernity then became a kind of scientific fundamentalism, sometimes called *scientism*, that excluded these other kinds of knowledge as non-scientific. Wilber calls this the 'great disaster of modernity' which, with the help of some of the greatest thinkers of our time, he describes as:

> the great nightmare of scientific materialism was upon us (Whitehead), the nightmare of one-dimensional man (Marcuse), the disqualified universe (Mumford), the colonisation of art and morals by science (Habermas), the disenchantment of the world (Weber) – a nightmare I have also called flatland.[6]

I was first drawn to the work of Wilber because spiritual ideas are central to his Integral Model, as he calls it. I had found that the few scholars who did attempt to bring spiritual ideas into the human/

social sciences were usually constrained by the need to bolt them on to the fringes of the established thinking of their disciplines, which invariably never worked very well. Wilber had no such constraints because he is not part of the 'academy' in the sense that he is not a university academic. Spirituality lies at the core of Wilber's thinking, and is one of the foundations of his philosophy and of the Integral Model. But Wilber's philosophy is very much more than a modern, western interpretation of traditional spiritual wisdom, though it certainly includes this. He distils the core ideas of postmodern thinking into three very important truths – constructivism, contextualism, and pluralism:

> constructivism means that the world we perceive is not simply given to us, it is partially constructed by us. Many – not all – of the things we thought were universal givens are really socially and historically constructed, and thus they vary from culture to culture. Contextualism points out that the meaning is context-dependent ... This gives interpretation a central place in our understanding of the world, because we do not simply perceive the world, we interpret it. And pluralism means that, precisely because meaning and interpretation are context-dependent – and there are always multiple contexts – then we should privilege no single context in our quest for understanding.[7]

It's difficult to pinpoint in time precisely when the established wisdom of modernity was superseded by the new truths of postmodernism. Some of the great philosophers of the late nineteenth and early twentieth centuries, such as Nietzsche and Husserl, were clearly thinking along these lines. But postmodernism would usually be considered a post-war phenomenon (WWII, that is), and probably not really established until the tumultuous 1960s. With the benefit of hindsight we can say that intellectually we have been in the postmodern era for at least fifty years, so that the 'new' truths of this era, that have rendered the 'old' truths of modernity obsolete, are really not all that new.

It follows from the three key truths of postmodernism identified by Wilber – constructivism, contextualism and pluralism – that the central flaw of modernity was the myth that there is any such thing as 100 per cent 'pure' objective knowledge. All human knowledge is *always* created and interpreted (socially constructed) through the subjective and intersubjective participation of the human knowers of that knowledge. Or to use the language of ancient spiritual wisdom, there is no knowing without a knower. No knowledge can ever be independent and free of subjectivity and a subjective knower. This is true even for the traditional 'hard' sciences of physics, chemistry and biology. It is especially true for the human sciences where the objects (or is it the subjects?) of enquiry are conscious human beings who have their own subjective experiences – that is, where the subjectivity of both the researcher and the researched are part of the research.

This brings us back to the self and subjectivity as an essential element of any research today, especially in the human sciences that seek to understand what it is to be human. If we limit our enquiry to just third-person data and knowledge then we will only ever achieve at best a partial understanding of whatever we might be studying. Wilber repeatedly points out that third-person knowledge is not so much incorrect as incomplete. In the postmodern era the first-person, subjective dimensions of all knowledge must at all times be part of the research agenda.

As I studied these ideas around postmodern thinking, I was drawn to the field known as Consciousness Studies, partly because it was saying interesting things about concepts of the self, but also because consciousness is often equated with spirit in some spiritual traditions. There has been a resurgence of interest in consciousness in the last decade or so that has brought together experts from a wide range of disciplines such as philosophy, neuroscience, psychology, cognitive science, computer science, cultural studies, and also the spiritual wisdom traditions. Although there is much that still remains mysterious about consciousness from a scientific standpoint, the current thinking about it introduces some exciting ideas about concepts of the self.

There is now a general acceptance in Consciousness Studies that the 'hard problem' of consciousness is that of *experience,* or the first-person, subjective, lived experience of any conscious phenomenon. The term 'hard problem' was coined by David Chalmers, an Australian philosopher at the forefront of Consciousness Studies, who called experience the hard problem to distinguish it from the 'easy' problem of a complete scientific understanding of the brain. The hugely complex and still largely unsolved problems of brain science are easy, in comparison, because at least 'we have a clear idea of how we might go about explaining them', says Chalmers. That is, we can be confident that the traditional scientific method is capable of (eventually) explaining the biology of the brain. But Chalmers and others have shown that these methods will *never* be able to explain consciousness adequately.[8]

The methods of traditional third-person science will never fully explain consciousness, because experience cannot be reduced to the third-person data required by these methods. The essential experiential data of consciousness are subjective, invisible and unmeasurable first-person data, which cannot be reduced to third-person data without losing their most important properties, which are the subjective *value and meaning* of an experience to those who live it. The reductive, third-person methods of traditional science will simply not help us to understand, describe and explain the first-person, lived experience of consciousness.

Many people in Consciousness Studies now feel that the only way to approach this 'hard problem' is to regard consciousness as an irreducible feature of the universe, like gravity or mass. Physics, for instance, does not attempt to dissect, analyse and reduce gravity into its component parts. Gravity is just a brute, irreducible fact of the universe, something that just *is*. Likewise with consciousness. A consequence of this is that if we wish to understand, describe and explain consciousness, then this will only ever be achieved by studying the first-person data, which in turn requires first-person methods of enquiry.

Although largely spurned by traditional third-person science, various first-person methods of research are available, such as phenomenology, heuristic and various narrative methods of enquiry, such as autoethnography. Of particular interest are the contemplative and meditative methods of the spiritual wisdom traditions, which can also be seen (through western scientific eyes) as first-person methods of enquiry. Chalmers highlights that 'our methods for gathering first-person data are quite primitive, compared to our methods for gathering third-person data … the former have not received nearly as much attention'. If we wish to understand consciousness – and the lived experience of any phenomenon – then we need to develop first-person methods enquiry to a level of sophistication that is comparable to our current third-person methods.

Consciousness Studies therefore reaches conclusions similar to the core ideas of contemporary postmodern thinking. Third-person knowledge, by itself, is not sufficient for a complete understanding of anything at all, but especially not of any humanly experienced phenomenon. Nothing is ever known without a knower or, more precisely, nothing is known without the act of knowing. Subjectivity is *always* involved in any knowledge and must be taken into consideration. Any scientific enquiry that limits itself to just the third-person data must now be seen in the postmodern era as partial and incomplete. Furthermore, the exclusion of first-person data and knowledge on the grounds that it is unscientific is now demonstrably ideological rather than rational (or indeed scientific).

Although the importance of first-person subjective experience is now mostly recognised and studied in most of the human and social sciences – with the notably curious exception of mental health – concepts of the self still remain confused and uncertain. David Chalmers, for instance, admits to not knowing what the self is and suggests that we 'throw away talk of the self and let's just look at the experiences themselves'.[9] In psychology we have moved from the divided self of Freud and James to the thoroughly deconstructed postmodern 'fragmented self'. Amid the confusion of so many scientific theories and taxonomies of the self, some postmodern commentators conclude that there is no such thing as the self, that it is not a useful concept, and therefore suggest that, like Chalmers, we should simply abandon our enquiry into it altogether. The problem with this, however, is that although subjective experience is now recognised, the self that subjectively experiences is nowhere to be found. At the turn of the twenty-first century we are hearing pronouncements of 'The Death of the Self in a Postmodern World',[10] an echo of Nietzsche's declaration of the death of God at the turn of the twentieth century.

Nietzsche's personal response to the death of God a hundred years ago has been described as a 'radical nihilism'. During the course of the twentieth century we have seen the widespread emergence of just such a nihilism, particularly in western cultures, and with it a profound sense of meaningless despair. Francisco Varela, a neuroscientist and eminent voice in Consciousness Studies, described this loss of God, and now the loss of self, at the centre of our existence as 'losing our grip on something familiar'.[11] The ground we stand on that used to seem so solid and familiar has been so thoroughly deconstructed that intellectually we now have to doubt whether we exist at all. At the very least, without a self (or God), no meaning or purpose to life seems possible. Perhaps the biological psychiatrists are right – our sense of self is just an illusion, a side effect, created by a bunch of meaningless neurons in a sea of meaningless neurotransmitters. Against this, of course, our sense of self not only persists but also remains important to us. How can we proceed past this intellectual impasse?

At this moment in our enquiry into the self, we find the ancient spiritual wisdom traditions have much to say that is useful. One of the reasons I find the current debates in Consciousness Studies so exciting is that they are one of the very few academic disciplines that have genuinely opened their doors to spiritual wisdom and spiritual ways of knowing. This is very challenging for some of the neuroscientists and others from the traditional 'hard' sciences, but in the spirit of genuine open enquiry they have recognised that spiritual ideas probably have something to offer, as they grapple with the hard problem of subjective experience. Commenting on the eastern meditative traditions, neuroscientist Francisco Varela observed that 'it would be a great mistake of western chauvinism to deny such observations as data and their potential validity'. Varela, sadly, died in 2001 but his colleagues continue his pioneering work of incorporating Buddhist mindfulness training into their research into human cognition. And David Chalmers, who is perhaps even more wary of the notion of spirit than he is of concepts of the self, recognises the potential value of spiritual ways of knowing:

I think the Buddhist traditions and other contemplative traditions have a lot to offer ... these guys have been studying subjective experience for many years from the inside, they've been gathering what we might call the first person data about the mind.[12]

Chalmers' interest remains in how the first-person data of subjective experience can contribute to our understanding of consciousness. Although he has the intellectual honesty to recognise that the contemplative spiritual traditions have something to offer in this enquiry, he still sees consciousness, not spirit (or God), as the source or site of subjective experience. But we seem to be getting very close to something resembling our sense of self as we experience it. Which in turn bears a strong resemblance to the notion of spirit that we find in many spiritual traditions. Chalmers also clings steadfastly to the assumption – and it is an assumption – that consciousness arises from the mind, that consciousness is a phenomenon of the mind. I find this assumption rather similar to the biological fundamentalism of modern psychiatry, only this time it is a kind of psychological fundamentalism that locates the self in the mind rather than the brain.

I find this intriguing, as it was Chalmers who identified subjective experience as the 'hard problem' of consciousness, precisely because it is so very different from all the other aspects of the mind that we study. I would argue with Chalmers that subjective experience, as the fundamental property of consciousness, is so unlike anything else that we think of as 'mental' that we need at least to entertain the possibility that it is not mental at all – that consciousness is not of the mind. Such a suggestion would clearly be provocative to many in Consciousness Studies, including Chalmers probably, because if it is not mental, and it's clearly not physical, then what could it be?

I don't want to just simply assert, like some dogmatic, religious ideologue, that the answer to this question is something we call 'spirit'. We need a better answer than that. I said that I was originally drawn to Consciousness Studies partly because consciousness is often equated with spirit in some spiritual traditions. I don't necessarily assume that spirit and consciousness are exactly equivalent, but it seems to me that consciousness as described by Chalmers and others is a lot closer to the notion of spirit in many spiritual traditions than it is to any notion of the mind. Consciousness, as a fundamental property of the universe, may be the 'something else' other than body and mind that spirituality speaks of and that Consciousness Studies suggests. At the very least, I see contemporary thinking in Consciousness Studies playing a key role in bridging the current gap between the wisdom of (objective, third-person) modern science and the equally valuable wisdom of the (subjective, first-person) spiritual traditions.

To conclude this Interlude, we return now to suicidology and the *Comprehensive Textbook of Suicidology* that insisted that suicidology must be 'as objective as it can, make careful measurements, count something'. The disdain for spiritual wisdom in this major reference exceeds even its disdain for first-person knowledge when it further states that '*suicidology has to have some observables*, otherwise it runs the danger of lapsing into mysticism and alchemy'. This is precisely the flatland science that Ken Wilber describes. The only other reference to spirituality in this supposedly comprehensive text of more than 600 pages is in the preface where the editors acknowledge 'the immense intellectual and spiritual debt that we all owe to our mentors and friends'.[13] It appears that spiritual needs and values play a part in the writing of a book but somehow are irrelevant to the study of suicide.

I'll finish with the words of Francisco Varela, who is so sadly missed, not only for his expansive wisdom and scholarly rigour but also his great eloquence. In the following quote he is referring to the need for first-person knowledge – the 'phenomenal realm' – in the study of consciousness and neuroscience. Given his efforts to bring spiritual ideas into his field of neuroscience, I am confident that he would agree that these words apply to the need also to bring spiritual ways of knowing into neuroscience, consciousness studies – and suicidology.

> to deprive our scientific examination of this phenomenal realm amounts to either amputating life of its most intimate domains, or else denying scientific explanatory access to it. In both cases the move is unsatisfactory.[14]

Notes

See the Further Reading section for more references to the topics of this Interlude. The specific references cited here are:

1. Bell, D (2001) Who is killing what or whom? Some notes on the internal phenomenology of suicide. *Psychoanalytic Psychotherapy, 15*(1): 21–37.
2. Maris, RW, Berman, AL & Silverman, MM (eds) (2000) *Comprehensive Textbook of Suicidology*. New York: Guilford Press, (pp. 62–3).
3. Sedikides, C & Brewer, MB (eds) (2001) *Individual Self, Relational Self, Collective Self.* Philadelphia, PA: Psychology Press.
4. Baumeister, RF (ed) (1999) *The Self in Social Psychology*. Philadelphia, PA: Psychology Press.

5. Prentice in Sedikides et al above.

6. Wilber, K (2000) *Integral Psychology: Consciousness, spirit, psychology, therapy.* Boston, MA: Shambhala, (p. 70).

7. Wilber, K (2000) *One Taste: Daily reflections on integral spirituality.* Boston, MA: Shambhala, (p. 152).

8. Chalmers, D (1995) Facing up to the problem of consciousness. *Journal of Consciousness Studies, 2*(3): 201.

9. This quote from Chalmers comes from an ABC radio interview, transcript available on the ABC website – www.abc.net.au/rn/science/mind/s919229.htm

10. This is the title of a chapter by Connie Zweig in Anderson, WT (ed) (1995) *The Truth About the Truth: De-confusing and re-constructing the postmodern world.* New York: Putnam Books.

11. Varela, FJ, Thompson, E & Rosch, E (1993) *The Embodied Mind: Cognitive science and human experience.* Cambridge, MA: MIT Press, (p. 130).

12. From the radio interview with Chalmers cited above.

13. Maris, RW, Berman, AL & Silverman, MM (eds) (2000) *Comprehensive Textbook of Suicidology.* New York: Guilford Press, (p. xx).

14. Varela, FJ & Shear, J (1999) First-person methodologies: What, why, how? *Journal of Consciousness Studies, 6*(2–3): 4.

5

Spiritual Self-Enquiry

To all deep thinking minds, the enquiry about the 'I' and its nature has an irresistible fascination. Call it by any name, God, Self, the Heart or the seat of Consciousness, it is all the same. The point to be grasped is this: that Heart means the very core of one's being, the centre without which there is nothing whatever.
  Ramana Maharshi

It was during one of my hospital detoxes that I woke up from a nap to find a grainy, black and white photo of this Indian-looking guy propped up beside my bed. I couldn't figure out who he was or how this photo had appeared there. I eventually guessed that it must have been left by a visitor, and probably by my long-time yoga buddy Susan. But I still had no idea who this guy was. A nurse confirmed that Susan had visited, found me asleep, sat with me for a while and left. She had also left a small booklet that went some way towards explaining the photo.

This was my introduction to Ramana Maharshi. Although it occurred quite early on in my 'four years of madness', I now regard this moment as the beginning of my recovery, though I had no sense of it at the time. Susan is one of my dearest friends and quite an Indiophile, visiting India regularly to nourish and maintain her spiritual equilibrium. We first met in the mid-1980s at a week-long yoga intensive that we had both decided to use as an occasion to give up smoking. At the front gate of the ashram (where smokers are banished to if they need to indulge their nasty habit) we met one day when Susan had run out of tobacco and I had run out of papers. An instant rapport was established and a beautiful friendship was born. Over the years I had become familiar with Susan bringing back her latest treasures from the spiritual supermarket that is India. These were not always my cup of tea but our sense of the spiritual was sufficiently similar that I usually found it worthwhile - and always great fun - to hear her latest stories of spiritual adventures and insights that she invariably came home with after each trip to India.

Bhagavan Sri Ramana Maharshi - to give him his full title, though I'll just call him Ramana from now - was the treasure Susan had brought home from her latest trip to India. This fellow, who died in 1950 (which explains the grainy photo), was my first introduction to a branch of yoga known as *gyan* yoga, or the yoga of self-enquiry. Although I had practised and studied yoga, irregularly and haphazardly, since the late 1970s, and had probably heard mention of gyan yoga, I knew next to nothing about it. Today I translate it as 'spiritual self-enquiry', and it was this that eventually set me free of my suicidality. But I'm getting ahead of my story ...

Initially, I was wary of this man in the photo. It looked too much like yet another guru from India and Susan knew very well that I was wary of the guru culture of yoga. My first serious encounter with yoga was when I was living in India in 1978, and I found that I loved the practices. Later, back in Melbourne after my Great Fire of London of 1979, and now a computer science student, I looked for a yoga school, thinking I knew what I wanted. I found one which taught a comprehensive and fairly traditional style of yoga, and said to the swami (the orange-robed, shaven-headed 'monks' of yoga) that I was looking for physical suppleness and relaxation. I can still see her lovely smile as she simply told me to think of it as a smorgasbord where I could sample the various practices and then take up whichever ones suited me. I might even have said that I didn't want any of the mystical crap, which is perhaps why she smiled so sweetly at me.

Over the next few years (the early 1980s) I was a pretty keen student of this yoga school. And, bit by bit, through the breathing, deep relaxation and meditation practices, along with the physical postures, a spiritual awareness began slowly to awaken within me. This was not some devotional, worshipping kind of spirituality. I was raised as, and had always been, a firm atheist (which remains true today) and would have run a mile at any of the devotional spirituality such as that of the Hare Krishna folk. No, the spirituality that emerged for me through these practices began with developing an awareness of the subtle 'energies' at work in the body, breath and mind. The starting point for this yoga is the physical body and the postures or exercises known as *asanas*, which is what most people think of as yoga. We then add to this an awareness of the breath and the specific breathing practices known as *pranayama,* to connect with the *prana* or subtle 'vital energy' (known as *ch'i* or *qi* in Chinese medicine). This yoga also had a deep relaxation practice known as *yoga nidra* or 'yogic sleep', and various meditation practices to develop a deeper awareness of the subtle aspects of body and mind. This work with body, breath and mind was my doorway into spirituality.

I loved these practices, and as an inquisitive, thoughtful kind of guy, I looked into the literature of yoga. This included not only the detailed explanations of the practices but also the philosophy of yoga, an ancient philosophy that has gone through many refinements over the centuries to give us the many diverse and sophisticated schools and traditions that we find in yoga today. It was all extremely stimulating and rewarding, so that over time I came to see myself as more of a spiritual being with a body, rather than the other way round. I can't put a date to this change in my thinking. It wasn't like some radical transformation - it happened very slowly, kind of organically, which was very nice. But I now lived in a richer, deeper world, and spirituality was central to that. This came about primarily through the practices, but the philosophy of yoga also became a cornerstone of my own personal philosophy.

I was sufficiently enchanted by yoga and this deepening awareness of my spiritual being to consider becoming a swami. I felt that my atheistic origins had thrown out the spiritual baby with the religious bathwater, and I had some catching up to do after thirty years of denial of my spirituality. The life of a swami was one where spiritual growth was constantly at the centre of every day, every activity, and for a while it was a very tempting possibility to consider.

I think there were two major reasons why I didn't follow the swami path back in the 1980s. The first was that I was still quite young, and at the start of an exciting and rewarding career in the computer software industry. My life in the 'straight' world was really very good and I mostly liked it. And my attachments to this world included my social life - in particular, the idea of the celibacy that came with swami-hood did not appeal to me. This was probably sufficient to save me from renouncing this world, but I also had one other major obstacle to swami life. This was my wariness about the guru culture. To become a swami you effectively swear allegiance to the guru - a kind of surrender to the guru. I had always had big problems with this as it seemed so fraught with danger. I was told that these problems were just my ego getting in the way, which is probably true enough. Thank heavens for my ego.

I think I'd already decided against the life of a swami when an awful scandal exploded at this yoga school that made the decision certain. It turned out that the most senior swami in Australia, who was revered and 'worshipped' as a semi-guru, had a weakness for young girls. I don't know all the details and wouldn't want to go into them here if I did. But it culminated in this fellow going to jail for a while and apparently he died a pretty sad, miserable and lonely death some years later. This scandal rocked the yoga school and many swamis left - there were more than two hundred in Australia at its peak, I believe. And of course the young girls and the families that had been abused by this guy were seriously wounded, some of them permanently. The school almost collapsed and disappeared in Australia, only resurfacing in the late 1990s.

It's painful for me to remember this horror because I still have a great appreciation, even love, for the teachings of yoga. But this terrible scandal confirmed and reinforced all my doubts about the guru culture. Blind obedience to an all-powerful 'master' was just too dangerous, too susceptible to corruption and abuse. Bad as this individual's behaviour was, I also saw that it was the whole culture that contributed to it. I was horrified to learn, much later, that there were quite a few swamis who knew of this man's paedophilia, but had remained silent. I even heard of one swami who I thought I knew quite well reassuring a fellow swami about the rumours that were going around before it exploded into the open by saying 'Don't worry, he won't get caught'. For me, this is exactly equivalent to the scandals surfacing in the churches today, and it's not due to a few rotten apples. It is systemic in such cultures. So I'm very glad that my ego stopped me from becoming a swami.

I'm also saddened by this scandal because I treasure ashram life as a place of spiritual refuge and sanctuary. At the start of my suicidal crisis I had talked with my sister about looking for some spiritual refuge where I might be able to attend to my despair. But I had lost touch with this yoga school, and as far as I was aware all their ashrams had been closed down. No other spiritual refuges or sanctuaries came to mind at the time. Recall that for a long time, as told in the 'drug detour' chapter, the advice I was receiving, and which I accepted, was to attend to my drug problem first - which brings us back to my hospital detox bed with this grainy photo of Ramana peering down at me.

When Susan next visited, I asked her to explain this photo - and I'll resume the story of Ramana shortly. But we also talked about what I might do after I got out of hospital. She told me that she'd heard that the ashram in the country not far from Melbourne that we used to go to had reopened to the public, and asked whether I might want to go there for a while after my detox. This was a scary thought. Neither Susan nor I had had anything to do with this school for nearly ten years, and the whole sorry story was a horrible memory. But I'd had good times at this ashram years earlier - the occasional weekend and a few week-long courses - and remembered it as a sacred and special space. Susan offered to find out more about whether it was possible to go there and how the place was being run, etc. I didn't have anywhere to go after the detox, which would finish in just a few days. Despite my reservations, the thought of taking refuge at the ashram was pretty appealing. Susan clinched it for me when she offered to take me up there and stay with me for the first week - and bring me back if I couldn't handle it.

It was a weird feeling as we approached the ashram in the car some ten years after our last visit. It had hardly changed at all. Surrounded by state forest, it was a beautiful setting. Susan escorted me in and we were greeted warmly by the swamis who ran the place. After these initial formalities, I was keen to visit the *sadhana* (spiritual practice) room where classes and other yoga sessions were held. As soon as I stepped inside it felt so familiar. These rooms acquire a very special feeling or mood that I just love. The big picture on the wall of the guru made me shudder a bit though, and I wondered whether I could go through with this. But the air of peace and calm in this room, so familiar and comfortable, felt like just what I was looking for - and needed.

I lived in the ashram for the next six months. It was a bit tough at first, adjusting to the routine. Up before dawn for a quick shower (and a smoke at the front gate) before class at 6.00 a.m., followed by breakfast, then the daily cleaning chores, which are followed by more chores. This constant 'work' at an ashram, whether it's cleaning, cooking, gardening, building repairs or working in the office is called *karma* yoga. Karma yoga, or the yoga of action (karma), aims to bring spiritual awareness to every activity you undertake, no matter how mundane. It is the yoga of selfless service where no reward is sought other than the opportunity to do the task itself. No tasks are better or more important than any other - cleaning the toilets is no more or less of an opportunity to practise karma yoga than, say, teaching a yoga class. Living in an ashram is to practise yoga every waking hour, and karma yoga takes up most of these hours. Although to the outside observer it can appear to be free labour for the ashram, karma yoga is its own distinct form of yoga, and a potent and effective one that can be fulfilling, rewarding and liberating.

Karma yoga is in fact one of the four major schools or traditions of yoga. The others are bhakti yoga, raja yoga and the gyan yoga already mentioned. Bhakti yoga is the yoga of devotion or worship. The simplest example of this is the Hare Krishna folk who worship the god Krishna, endlessly chanting his name. At this ashram we also practised bhakti yoga regularly, mainly through the chanting to music called *kirtan*. When I first encountered kirtan I was uneasy about it, but once I accepted it as just another yoga practice rather than some worship of god or guru, I slowly learned to appreciate it as another of the delights of yoga. At the ashram I even learned to play the harmonium (a kind of musical squeeze-box with a piano-like keyboard), which was a big adventure for this musical klutz.

Raja yoga includes the yoga that most of us think of when we hear the word yoga. Raja means 'king', so raja yoga is the yoga of kings - though I also translate this, with some Aussie irreverence perhaps, as the yoga that even a king can do. It includes the practices of asanas or postures, pranayama or breathing practices, pratyahara or deep relaxation, and the various 'meditation' practices. These we did mostly in the regular morning classes but we also had a daily deep relaxation before lunch and regular meditations in the evenings. And in between all these ... more karma yoga.

Gyan yoga did not, however, feature much in the teachings of this school or in the life of this ashram. Despite all my years of yoga I had hardly heard of it, and knew next to nothing about it - until

Susan gave me Ramana's photo and the little booklet. The booklet, *Nan Yar* or *Who Am I?*, is basically a dialogue between Ramana and a spiritual seeker who came to see him some time 'about the year 1902'. Maybe the reason gyan yoga is not often taught in yoga schools is that there are no real teachings. Gyan yoga works through dialogues that enquire into the nature of the self. In India these dialogues are known as *satsang*, which roughly translates into an assembly (*sangha*) to discuss truth or reality (*sat*). Another translation I like is 'to assemble in (the presence of) truth'.

When I first looked at this booklet while still in the hospital detox I'd assumed it would be pretty much more of the same sort of thing that I had read so much of over the last decade or so. But it seemed to have something more, or slightly different, and I found myself picking it up again and again during my time at the ashram. My copy is just fifteen pages, so it was easy to read over and over. And each time I read it I seemed to find something more in it. Initially I didn't see it as the radical (non-)teaching that I do today. It was more like just another nuance on the vast literature of yoga that I was already reasonably familiar with. I picked it up in quiet moments in the busy routine of ashram life and I guess that, bit by bit, I incorporated some of the ideas from this tiny text into my meditations. And, remember, I was desperately seeking some way out of my pain that, despite the wonderful ashram life, was still very present deep within me.

But the penny didn't drop, so to speak, while I was living at the ashram. I had accepted without question the prevailing view that this peculiar thing called 'enlightenment' was an impossible dream for ordinary folk such as myself. The teachings of yoga seemed quite clear on this. Enlightenment required many years of diligent and dedicated practice, the strict observance of a severe moral code, and also the blessing of an already enlightened guru who at some point might - just might - tap you on the shoulder and give you the much sought after 'transmission' of enlightenment. And all of this would take many lifetimes. In almost all the spiritual circles I have had some contact with, the message was always that it was presumptuous to expect or anticipate enlightenment in this life. So it was clearly not something that was on the agenda for someone like me, who could not possibly follow such a strict and disciplined life. For me, this actually became an argument in favour of suicide. I had clearly messed up this life so why not just move on to the next one.

Although mostly dormant while at the ashram, my inner chaos quickly surfaced whenever I stepped out of this safe space. Towards the end of my time at the ashram I had a few visits to Melbourne, where I couldn't resist picking up the heroin again. It was bizarre. I was now very healthy and even cheerful and there was certainly no physical addiction to the heroin. But outside the safety and sanctuary of the ashram, I found the emptiness inside me was too hard to bear and I almost automatically took refuge in the heroin. I was only ever away for a day or so, so there was no time to run up any sort of serious habit. And as soon as I was back in the ashram the urge for heroin pretty much disappeared straight away and was not a problem.

During these visits to Melbourne I encountered the other spiritual teacher or guide who, along with Ramana, was to be so vital to my recovery - an American woman called Gangaji. Her American name is Antoinette Varner, but she was given the name Gangaji by her own teacher-guide, an Indian chap by the name of H.W.L. Poonja, but affectionately known as just Papaji. Papaji had spent time with, and was a follower (I'm personally uncomfortable with the word devotee or disciple) of Ramana. He later carried on Ramana's tradition of satsang in Lucknow in north India, where my friend Susan met him and spent time in satsang with him on a couple of her visits to India. Papaji gave Antoinette the name Gangaji in 1990 and told her to take satsang to the West. She is now an eloquent, contemporary, Western voice of this lineage of satsang.

Towards the end of 1996, before finally leaving the ashram, I had heard a few of Susan's tapes of satsang with Gangaji, and I liked what I heard. I was still regularly dipping into *Nan Yar* and still finding new treasures each time I did. Gangaji helped me see more clearly what Ramana was saying, and the radical nature of this teaching was starting to become apparent. Next thing I knew, Gangaji was coming to Australia and Susan roped me into being a volunteer at the satsang being scheduled for her visit. When the time came, I went to Melbourne, immediately started using heroin again and attended all of Gangaji's satsang rather stoned on heroin. I also signed up for a week-long retreat with Gangaji in Murwillumbah but my heroin use was out of control by the time I got there. This was the retreat where I made the pathetic, almost comical, attempt to cut myself with a twin-blade 'safety' razor. This retreat was not a big success for me.

I returned briefly to the ashram after yet another detox, now with my daily anti-depressants in my pocket. But I was ready to leave, as I felt that I had got what I could out of the ashram and wanted to move on. Perhaps I should have stayed. Who can tell what might have happened if I had? I certainly felt safe and happy there, but I think I didn't want to feel that I was confined to this sanctuary for my safety. And the opportunity arose to go and live with some dear friends in the hills inland from mid-coast New South Wales.

I spent all of 1997 in the hills with these friends. For me it was rather idyllic in a very rustic kind of way. My friends had just bought some land that they wanted to develop into a community and were happy for me to live there. Under one condition. No heroin. I agreed and for a year I didn't take any heroin at all. This was the year on the Aropax anti-depressant and the regular counselling with Phil. I worked pretty hard, helping to make the run-down buildings habitable, establishing gardens, and so on, but also taking many long walks in the beautiful forest on and around this property. But as at the ashram, I was still hiding from the world here - a beautiful, safe and healthy place to hide, but it was still hiding nevertheless. I didn't socialise much with others in the local village, and was happy just to continue my karma yoga practice, this time on the numerous chores at my friends' property.

It was while living here that I said to a friend that I couldn't see any way out of my internal chaos without a change in consciousness comparable to the change that occurs in puberty, a change that I was unable to imagine - prophetic words, but not much consolation at the time. Instead, I tried to convince myself that this inner sadness and emptiness was just the human condition and that I had to accept this and get used to it. I tried - I feel I tried so very hard - to accept and adjust to this, so that I might 'move on', and perhaps eventually find some joy and meaning again with this acceptance. But I never did. If I thought about it (which I tried not to) I hated it and just kept on hiding. Until the end of that year when I moved on out of this home in the forest and the worst year of my four years of madness began.

Previous chapters have told of this horrible year so I'll jump to early 1999, when I had just been discharged from the lockup at Royal Park after my last (and final) serious suicide attempt. I was about to start 'therapy' with the psychiatrist who wanted to bully me into submission with his undisclosed diagnoses of sado-masochism and personality disorder. After a week or so of 'couch surfing' at the homes of friends and family, a space came up in a rooming house in North Fitzroy. It is impossible to overstate how important this rather meagre living space was to be for me. This tiny room, in a house with eleven other strangers, each of whom had their own 'issues', was a godsend. My very own few square metres of space that I could call 'home'. I lived there for four years, and am forever indebted to this tiny little patch of the planet that was a safe, clean, affordable and secure home for me.

During my year in NSW, I had continued to read and reread my little booklet, but I also now had a bigger book of Ramana's satsang, *The Teachings of Bhagavan Sri Ramana Maharshi In His Own Words*, edited by Arthur Osborne. This became a treasure trove, and remains my favourite reference today, though *Nan Yar* will forever be special. I had also, during the eight months in the zombie-land of the Methadone, Efexor and Zyprexa, attended the Gangaji video satsang held in private homes in Melbourne. With Ramana as the source and Gangaji as a clear voice that spoke my language, the pieces of the jigsaw that were to save my life started coming together. Not that I noticed at the time, though.

The essence of these teachings – which Gangaji called a 'non-teaching' – is that the fundamental spiritual question is 'Who am I?' The second, and only other 'lesson' of this teaching is that the answer to this question is to be found in silence. That's it. That's all you need to know – there's nothing more to it. All the rest of any enquiry – and many other questions do get asked in satsang – will always return to these two basic 'truths' of self-enquiry. Even the tiny *Nan Yar* booklet was repetitive in constantly returning to these two fundamental truths.

These teachings are not something that you can study and learn and practise like other yoga teachings, which is why Gangaji calls them a non-teaching (though she happens to be one of the most gifted 'teachers' I've ever had). Chanting Who-am-I, Who-am-I, Who-am-I like some mantra will not help. All that is required is that this question 'Who am I?' becomes the most important issue in your life. If fame or fortune or any other desire, such as the desire for that perfect job, house, holiday or lover, are more important for you then fine, pursue these first. But should the time come that this question arises for you as *the* critical issue in your life, then self-enquiry says attend to it - fully, earnestly, ruthlessly and without compromise. I eventually saw this as precisely the crisis of the self that I had been struggling with for four years.

Gangaji talks of these (non-)teachings as an invitation. For those for whom this 'Who am I?' question arises with compelling urgency, self-enquiry is an invitation to 'wake up' and realise the Self, the spiritual self. It is the invitation Gangaji received from her teacher, Papaji, who received it from Ramana, and which she is now simply passing on to anyone willing to receive it. But she also points out that this invitation comes from the Self. From your true Self within you that is inviting you into a deeper awareness and appreciation of your being. It is, to use Gangaji's simple eloquence, 'your true self calling you home'. These evocative words resonated powerfully for me. I recognised that I had always felt homeless within myself, and here it was being suggested that there was a safe and peaceful 'home' already within my being that was waiting for me, waiting for me to come home. And my pain and yearning were a simple call to 'come home'.

But I couldn't just accept what Ramana and Gangaji were saying simply because these wonderful people were saying it. I was sceptical of all gurus and wary of the hype that you typically found around the idea of 'enlightenment'. My busy and 'clever' western intellectual mind searched hard for some flaw in their reasoning and the arguments they were making. But I was having trouble finding them. And, despite the elegant simplicity of what they were saying, I got bogged down on just *how* you might make the transition to this very simple awakening. That is, in one way it seemed all too easy and therefore not credible. But on the other hand, it was all too impossibly hard because *how* do you surrender to this silence of the Self? Clearly it was not some deliberate decision that you make like deciding to apply for a job ... or kill yourself. I struggled with this for a couple of years before I finally 'understood' just how easy it really was to just be me. It was an ugly couple of years, but what a treasure there was waiting for me!

*   *   *   *   *

Some years after my recovery, a friend challenged me when I said that spirituality was not at all religious for me. In particular, he challenged my claim that spirituality was not at all faith-based for me. He insisted that somewhere in my spirituality there must ultimately be some faith belief. It may not be faith in God, he argued, but still, somewhere, some sort of faith – in something – was a necessary part of any spirituality. It was a good point and a challenging question. It forced me to look at my understanding of spirituality to see if I could find the faith belief he was insisting must be there somewhere.

Talking it through with him, my answer began with the observation that if we looked at religious faith, for instance, then faith in God is really just the most fundamental assumption of all systems of religion. That is, religious faith is the assumption that God exists even though this cannot be proved to our senses or explained rationally. This faith in God, the assumption that a God of some kind exists, is the bedrock on which all the other religious beliefs are then constructed. So I said to my frowning friend that although my sense of the spiritual does not assume the existence of any God, there was perhaps a similar sort of bedrock assumption to my understanding of spirituality. This is the assumption that I exist. Or at least, that I seem to exist. If I think about it, this assumption that I exist – that 'I am' – is really quite mysterious to me. But, as far as I can tell, I do seem to exist.

Spiritual self-enquiry confronts this mystery that 'I' seem to exist when it says that the ultimate spiritual question is 'Who Am I?' We saw in the Interlude that contemporary thinking about concepts of the self – about our sense of self – is rather inadequate and unsatisfactory. We are certainly not the biochemical robots that modern biological psychiatry would have us believe we are. Nor does modern psychology with its dissection of the self into many selves quite satisfy the sense of self that we experience as unified, whole and continuous. And postmodern ideas of the self are similarly fragmented with their narrative self of many stories, but without the self that is the story-teller anywhere in sight. Can spiritual enquiry into our sense of self take us beyond this impasse?

Spirituality is almost as difficult to talk about as suicide.

Whenever my PhD is mentioned, I'm often asked what my topic was and when I say 'suicide' I can often see a look of apprehension in people's eyes at the mention of this taboo word. If I then say, 'and spirituality', then the look in their eyes can change from apprehension to suspicion, as I see them step back in anticipation of some spiritual sales-pitch. Suicide is scary, but spiritual zealots can sometimes be even scarier.

Another problem in discussing spirituality is that many people see it as supernatural, magical, irrational, delusional, unreal, or at least 'unscientific'. I once heard a psychiatrist try ever so hard to be respectful of religious beliefs by calling them *benign* delusions, to contrast them to the delusions that he usually diagnosed as mental illness. Although spiritual ways of knowing, almost by definition, take us beyond the rational mind, this does not mean that it is impossible to talk sensibly and rationally about spiritual values, spiritual needs and spiritual ways of knowing. On the contrary, this conversation is urgently needed if we are to move beyond the shallow, simplistic understanding of our sense of self that we find in current thinking about suicide.

Yet another obstacle to a discussion of spirituality is the distinction between spirituality and religion, which is more than just my friend's insistence that all spirituality must be based on some sort of 'act of faith'. My short answer to this is that it is quite possible and indeed very common to be spiritual without being at all religious – and vice versa. I was raised an atheist and remain an atheist today. But religion is not just about belief in a God. Religion is best understood as institutionalised spirituality, a social construction or cultural artefact superimposed over our intrinsic spirituality in a similar way that we superimpose maps of nations over the intrinsic geography of the earth. At their best, religions give a social and cultural structure to the expression of our spirituality, creating spaces where our spirituality can be studied, taught, practised, shared and celebrated. And like the many different languages of nations, there are many different 'languages' for the religious expression of our spirituality. At their best, religions are the schools and sanctuaries of spiritual life.

At their worst, however, religions have all too often become political institutions that have lost contact with their spiritual origins and responsibilities. I cannot see any genuine spirituality in a religion that claims their god is the one true god and, what's more, that they are prepared to kill anyone who thinks otherwise. For many of us, the long and still continuing history of all sorts of terrible abuses in many religions means that they have little credibility at all as spiritual institutions. It is certainly possible to be religious without being at all spiritual. Religions have also not responded well to the challenges of science. When science began to demonstrate the folly of some core religious teachings, religions tried to respond by dogmatically asserting their political power rather than honestly engaging with this new knowledge. Religions plainly lost these debates, and have been in decline ever since, at least in the western world.

A further difficulty with spirituality is the lack of any clear, agreed definition of what it means. One definition that I first heard many years ago is a simple but useful one to keep in mind for our spiritual enquiry into our sense of self. It simply says that spirituality is those aspects of our being that are *neither physical nor mental.* I'd like to add to this that for me spirituality is very personal and very much of this world. It is about my deepest sense of self as I experience it in the world in which I live, and nothing at all to do with faith in God or any 'other world' supernatural beliefs.

With all these awkward hazards in any discussion of spirituality behind us, we now return to the spiritual self-enquiry that set me free of my suicidality. As described in the narrative, the primary reference for me in this enquiry is the teachings of Ramana Maharshi. For those with academic inclinations, this chapter is sort of on the 'theory' of self-enquiry rather than its 'methods' – i.e. the *what* rather than the *how*. This is a bit of an artificial distinction because self-enquiry is not a typical spiritual teaching based around doing certain practices in order to get particular results. But the path of self-enquiry has some obstacles that need to be cleared away before we can fall into the embrace of our spiritual Self.

Spiritual self-enquiry begins with the question 'Who am I?'. Ramana is then quite emphatic that this question cannot be answered in or by the mind. This immediately presents us with a major obstacle, especially those of us whose sense of self is intimately tied up with our mental world, our mental or psychological sense of self. Which is most of us, I think, and in particular people like me who have spent many years in the education system of a secular, western culture. I call this obstacle to self-enquiry the Cartesian Myth because it the mistaken belief that I am who I *think* I am. But we must not take this to be so just because Ramana says so far less because *I* do. Self-enquiry demands a ruthless investigation into your own experience of your sense of self. We will do a little of this soon but it actually helps to know the answer to the 'Who am I?' question in advance.

Ramana is equally emphatic that the answer to 'Who am I?' is silence. Which is pretty much the beginning and the end of the theory of self-enquiry. That's all there is to it. The question is 'Who am I?' and the answer is silence. For a few lucky people this may be all that needs to be heard to grasp all that self-enquiry has to teach, and to fall effortlessly into the embrace of the spiritual Self. For most of us though, it's not quite that easy. Obstacles remain. The first obstacle to silence is the busy, noisy mind that is sometimes described as like a tree full of monkeys. And along with all this noise, a further obstacle to recognising the Self in silence is the mind's tenacious clinging to the myth that we are who we think we are. So before we can look more closely at the silent Self that is waiting so patiently to receive us, we must first enquire into the nature of the mind, of which Ramana succinctly states:

Apart from thoughts, there is no such thing as mind.

This simple statement is Ramana's radical challenge to modern psychology and how most of us think of the mind. We typically think of the mind as a part of us that is always with us. But if we think carefully about it, Ramana is quite correct. What we call the mind is nothing other than the presence of thoughts. More precisely, the experience of having a mind is to consciously experience the presence of thoughts. Note that the word 'thoughts' here means not just the cognitive mind but includes the emotional mind of our feelings. There is debate about whether feelings are just particular kinds of thoughts or vice versa but I'm agnostic on this debate and use the word thoughts here to include both.

Another possible problem with this definition of the mind is that it doesn't consider unconscious or subconscious minds. I would call these metaphorical concepts of mind that uses the language of thoughts and feelings to describe the unseen influences on our conscious thoughts, feelings and behaviour. Like all good metaphors, it can be useful as a tool to explore the invisible origins and motivations behind our conscious life in meaningful, human language – i.e. the language of thoughts and feelings. It is therefore a metaphor that is widely used, and often very effectively, in many forms of psychotherapy. But the metaphorical 'unconscious/ subconscious mind' is not the mind that Ramana and I are exploring in spiritual self-enquiry, which is the conscious lived experience of the presence of thoughts and feelings.

You may not agree with this understanding of the mind but that is actually not too important, though in the spirit of self-enquiry I do encourage you to investigate for yourself whether you can find any other satisfactory definition. But with this understanding of the mind, the next critical step in spiritual self-enquiry is to enquire into what Ramana calls the 'I' thought, or the 'I' in the 'Who am I?' question. When we do this, we find that the 'I' thought has a very special status among all the thoughts that we might have. In Ramana's words:

> Of all the thoughts that arise in the mind, the 'I' thought is the first. It is only after the rise of this that the other thoughts arise.

Our enquiry so far has been basically a psychological one in that we are using the mind to explore the mind. It can help sometimes to ask this question in a variety of ways. Who or what within me does the 'I' thought refer to? Or what can I find within me that comes before or lies behind or beneath the 'I' thought? On every occasion, whatever thoughts you might have about these questions soon become just more thoughts. And always, every one of these thoughts contains the question, 'who am I that is having these thoughts?' Yes, it can truly put your mind in a spin, as any thought that you might have will always lead you back to that very first thought – 'Who am I?' Eventually, hopefully, you will abandon the search for the self in the mind.

Most people, like me, will probably not be persuaded to abandon the search for the self in the mind simply because Ramana or anyone else urges us to. Only your own personal realisation of the futility of this search – through your own personal self-enquiry – will persuade you. This is the ruthless obligation of self-enquiry. You must enquire, deeply, honestly, ruthlessly; and not be persuaded by anything other than your own direct experience of whatever you find through your enquiry. For most people, like me, the mind will cling tenaciously to more and more thoughts, more and more explanations, more and more stories about who you are. But in the end, we are always left with the question, who am I, the thinker, the explainer, the story-teller?

Realising that the mind is simply unable to answer this most urgent question can be a disturbing, even frightening, moment in our self-enquiry. If we have lived our lives believing that the self is in and of the mind, then this realisation can represent a serious threat to our sense of self. We may not have altogether lost our mind at this point but we can feel that we have lost our self, which can be distressing. It is wise to be cautious and gentle with yourself at these difficult times, which we will look at further in the next chapter. But for now, we can take reassurance from the teachings of Ramana, and all the great spiritual sages throughout history, that what lies beyond the mind is not something to be feared. On the contrary, a great treasure awaits us. And for me, this treasure set me free of my urge to die.

Once we abandon our search for the self in the mind then all we are left with is empty silence – or silent emptiness. The space from which all thoughts arise and into which they will all subside. A space where there is no thought, no thing, no sound, no image, no shape. Only silence, complete utter empty silence. This is the silence that Ramana urges us to pay attention to. This is the silence in which the spiritual Self can be found and met. And the key to attending to this silence – to approach it, to become intimate with it, to embrace it and be embraced by it, to 'know' it – is to quieten the mind.

Quietening the mind is the purpose of all meditation practices. But for many of us, quietening the mind is not so easy. The incessant chatter of our busy minds, that tree full of monkeys, is persistent and tenacious. So there are practices we can do to help us connect with and spend time in those brief moments of silence between the hectic coming and going of our thoughts. We tend to be preoccupied with our thoughts so that we typically overlook these moments, this space, between our thoughts. I particularly like the idea of meditation as looking at our thoughts as clouds passing in the sky. During meditation, we turn our attention to the sky rather than the clouds, to the silence between the thoughts.

In the next chapter we look further at meditation and other spiritual practices. But Ramana cautions us against spiritual practice becoming its own obstacle to spiritual awakening – i.e. self-realisation, or realising the spiritual Self in silence. This brings us to another radical challenge in his teachings, similar to his challenge to the orthodoxy of modern psychology and the Cartesian Myth that we are who we think we are. Only this time he challenges an orthodoxy found in many spiritual traditions, and certainly one that I had learned through yoga.

I had learned through yoga that the goal of spiritual practice was enlightenment. But I had also learned that for someone like me this was an impossible dream, so impossible that it even became another argument for suicide. Attaining enlightenment required diligent practice, a rather severe moral code, the blessing of the guru, and many lifetimes, all of which taught me that it was way beyond my reach; and presumptuous to even imagine that it might be possible in this life.

Ramana's radical challenge to this common orthodoxy is that so-called enlightenment is nothing other than to realise the truth of who you already are, *right now*. In particular, he stresses that self-realisation, which is another common but much better term for spiritual awakening than enlightenment, is not something new to be attained or acquired:

> Realisation already exists; no attempt need be made to attain it. For it is not anything external or new to be acquired. It is always and everywhere – here and now, too.

I had learned that enlightenment was something 'over there' that I had to do all these impossible things in order to reach, acquire or attain. Enlightenment was something external, separate and distant to the life I lived, the self I lived. I now call this the Enlightenment Myth which, like the Cartesian Myth that locates the self in the mind, is another mistaken belief that locates the self somewhere other than where it is. And Ramana was adamant that it is these false ideas that are the only obstacle to realising the self:

> No one is ever away from the Self and therefore everyone is in fact Self-realised; only – and this is the great mystery – people do not know this and want to realise the Self. Realisation consists only in getting rid of the false idea that one is not realised. It is not anything new to be acquired.

As with his challenge to the Cartesian Myth, I struggled with Ramana's radical challenge to the Enlightenment Myth. It was a shock. Here was this man, widely recognised as one of the great spiritual sages of the modern era, saying that this common understanding of the goal of spiritual practice was false, a mistaken belief, a lie. In some ways this was perhaps even more shocking than his equally radical challenge to the other common understanding that the self can be found in and by the mind. But it was also potentially great news for me. It opened up the possibility of finding something beyond my persistent suicidality, perhaps the peace that I was yearning for like a drowning man yearns for air. It created a space where something other than the meaningless, constant pain of suicidal psychache might be possible.

But being persuaded by a convincing argument is not self-realisation. The struggle continued. Getting rid of these 'false ideas' turns out to be not so easy, at least not for someone like me. It can seem that without any of these false ideas at all there is then no self at all. This is uncannily similar to the conclusions reached by some postmodern thinkers who, after exhaustive analysis of our many selves, decide that none of them is real. And then declare the 'death of the self', an echo of Nietzsche's declaration of the death of God a hundred years earlier. This conclusion remains unsatisfactory though. Not only does it conflict with our sense of self as we live it; such a conclusion can also be quite distressing. And like Nietzsche, we can be left with little more than a nihilistic despair. For those of us who might already be feeling suicidal, this can be not only distressing but dangerous.

Our self-enquiry is on a knife edge now. Our ruthless, exhaustive enquiry into the self has yielded nothing that we can get a handle on. On the contrary, everything that we might have once clung to for some possible hope has been debunked (deconstructed) as false. We are left clinging to a fast-sinking raft not unlike the postmodern dead-end, with no self and nowhere to go. Now that all these possibilities are finally exhausted, it is time to turn to all that is left. Silence.

And so finally we come face to face with the silence that Ramana has been pointing to from the very outset. The silence of no mind, no thoughts. Stepping into this silence and embracing it as myself – my spiritual Self – set me free. But this tiny step is also a huge step because it is to surrender to the unknowable mystery of the silence at the very heart of our being.

6

The Willingness to Surrender

The time will come when you will have to stop with all the stories.
Gangaji

I cannot point to a single day or moment when all the pieces of the self-enquiry jigsaw fell into place, and peace and freedom arrived. But I can pinpoint it roughly to the first week of June, 1999. I shed my suicidality (and my heroin addiction) like a snake shedding a no-longer-useful skin. I found that instead of hiding from the world as I had for the previous four years, I now wanted to 'walk in the world again'. These were the actual words that I found myself saying to myself. And it was almost alarming. It was certainly quite an alien feeling after years of hiding from the world. And the key to this radical change was the realisation that at the core of my being was a bottomless, timeless peace - a peace that I now also recognised as everything that I had been yearning for all my life.

In this peace I also found a great freedom, the other keyword of this radical transformation. This peace and freedom have remained with me ever since. The peace is the silent stillness of who I truly am at the core of my being, and the freedom is the freedom to be just me - nothing more and nothing less.

This ever so slight but also radical shift in consciousness was also very, very funny. Gangaji tells the story of a woman who described this liberation as being picked up and turned right side up after a lifetime of walking around on her hands. Her first reaction to this was an extraordinary sense of relief at how easy it was to get around now on her feet rather than on her hands. 'So that's what these feet are for!' she exclaimed. And then came the embarrassment of realising that she had had these feet all along. The delight of discovering her feet, though, was so much more than the embarrassment that all she could do was laugh at herself.

My own version of this tale is that I now saw that, prior to June 1999, my inner 'home' had always been one of sadness. Despite the many wonderful adventures of my life, the place that I always seemed to return to in the privacy of my inner self was a sad place. I was walking on my hands. Sometimes I was able to do this quite skilfully, at other times rather clumsily, and then sometimes I fell over. To realise the peace of the spiritual self as my new inner 'home' was to be put right side up. And how utterly easy it now became to walk in the world again. And how embarrassing it was to see how clumsily I had struggled all these years. I felt like a complete dope! But all I could do was laugh at the joy of it ... and I've been laughing joyously ever since.

It's difficult to say for sure exactly what all the steps were that took me to this joyous peace and freedom. With the benefit of hindsight I can say that it felt like the pieces of the jigsaw were slowly jiggling into place, but identifying all the pieces in this puzzle is not so easy. Obviously I acknowledge the wisdom of Ramana and the eloquence of Gangaji as crucial, but these teachings by themselves do not set you free. Waking up to the Self is not some cognitive decision that you take or something that you study in books and then sit an exam. It is a change of consciousness comparable to the change that occurs during puberty, as I had unknowingly predicted years before. How does this happen? What can we do to help make it happen? What are the other pieces of the jigsaw that might allow this to occur?

For me, I can say that the key 'event' was that I surrendered. Once again, I cannot pin down some critical moment when this surrender took place. Nor can I say exactly what I mean by surrender. I can say that it was definitely not some decision that I carefully took and then went ahead and deliberately did it. In many ways it was simply a 'letting go', and that the main obstacle to this was my clinging to something that was holding me back. At the time it was certainly not clear what I was clinging to, nor what I needed to surrender to. Surrender was a step into the unknown or, more accurately, into the unknowable. And there was great resistance to this. I guess it was fear.

There were several pieces to my jigsaw at the time that I am sure were important for this surrender to occur. First, I was living in the rooming house in North Fitzroy, which gave me a physical 'home' that was clean and safe. As I have said, the importance of this cannot be overstated. Next, I did take the very deliberate decision to get off the Methadone and all the crazy psycho-medications. I was not prepared to live any longer in this drugged stupor, I would rather die than continue like this. One or the other, it didn't matter much to me which.

As I weaned myself off all the drugs, I found that I had the urge to start the day with a long walk. I've never been much of a walker for the sake of walking, but each day I was getting up at around dawn and walking around North Fitzroy for an hour or more. I was unable to do more demanding physical exercise - remember, I was now twenty kilos overweight and basically a fat, lazy slug. But, for some peculiar reason, I just wanted to walk and walk and walk these mornings. This unusual behaviour for me somehow also seems significant for the recovery that was now just around the corner, though still not yet visible.

It was around this time, when I was also detoxing off the Methadone, that I found I simply could not put another Zyprexa tablet into my mouth - ever again! This was another piece of the jigsaw leading up to my surrender, when I suddenly realised I was the most drug-free that I'd been in years. For more than two years I had been taking a pretty hefty dose of prescribed medications and/or heroin, and now I had stopped, and they had also finally washed out of my system. Drug free! What a radical thought - or so it seemed to me. And in this fleeting, unexpected moment, there was a feeling of being flung into some new space as though out of a slingshot. I can't say it any better than this, because this is how it felt and this was the language I used to describe it at the time. And it made me laugh.

Another piece of the jigsaw was that I had effectively walked away from the doctors. I was finished with both addiction and 'depression' as explanations for my suicidality. Neither made any sense to me now. And the various treatments I had received in some way confirmed this because they had not helped at all - in fact, they had made things worse. So I was finished with all the doctors who were only able to 'treat' me on the basis of these useless diagnoses.

As all these pieces started to come together, I started feeling on top of that wave described earlier, the one which was maybe taking me somewhere good but which might also crash me onto the rocks. I had the option to pull out of this wave, or so it seemed to me, but despite the risks and the advice I received at the time, I chose not to.

As far as I can tell, this was my moment of surrender. I turned my back on the doctors, ignored my own mind, trusted my heart - and rode that wave. I still didn't have a clue where it might be taking me, and I still felt that it was risky. And I still felt that I could pull out and avoid the 'crash' if I chose. But I trusted it, and made a quite deliberate decision to let it take me. Even if that was to my death.

I emphasise that this is only my best guess of that moment of surrender. The fruits of this surrender were still not obvious yet, or at least not in any enduring kind of way. It was too soon. It was only a few weeks since my last heroin, and not much longer than that since my last half-hearted suicide attempt, when I had yet again tried to jump from a high place and found that I couldn't do it. Doubts persisted. My life was still a mess in many ways. I'd had four years of this madness and a few days or weeks of this wave were not going to convince even me, despite the confidence I felt in it, that everything was now hunky-dory.

As it turned out, there have been no rocks. The wave took me to the peace and freedom that I enjoy today. But there was more - much more - to the circumstances surrounding and leading up to this moment.

Another essential ingredient to my surrender was that I was totally exhausted. Physically, mentally and emotionally, I was at a dead-end. I had struggled for four years to try and find a way to live with myself and had found nothing. Sure, I had done some clumsy and stupid things in the process, such as all the heroin I'd taken and the suicide attempts. But I really felt that, unlike in 1979, I had tried so very hard - again and again and again. And nothing had worked, or even come close. Drug rehab and AA/NA hadn't worked. All the efforts of the doctors, psychiatrists and psychologists hadn't achieved anything. Living at the ashram had been nice, but I left there as sad as I had arrived. Likewise with living with my friends in the bush in NSW. Family and friends, who had supported me so bravely, were also not enough. All my worst fears were being confirmed. I was just unable to live in this skin. It was too hard, too painful and nowhere near worth it. Four years of this had drained me of whatever strength I might have had. Or so it felt. It was more than just personal exhaustion. I also felt that I'd exhausted all possibilities of ever finding any sort of hope.

Another significant factor was the feeling that I was somehow not allowed to die. I don't want to overstate this, as it has connotations of some god or Higher Power that is calling the shots, and I don't feel that at all. It was more like I just felt I was such a total misfit and failure that I couldn't even kill myself. The overdose in mid-98 should have killed me, goddamit! It was a massive overdose, at least as big as the one of the Great Fire in 1979. But somehow my physical constitution, which has more than once been described as the proverbial 'brick shithouse', showed itself to be stronger than my efforts to snuff it out. Back in 1980 one of my sisters had said to me, 'Dave, you've got more lives than a cat but I want you to slow down 'cos you're running out'. Well, apparently not. There was a feeling that somewhere inside me, somehow, there was a life-force that was stronger than my power to snuff it out. I had even talked about this with Nicky, who pointed out that it was possible to override this life-force with will-power so I shouldn't assume that it was impossible for me to kill myself.

The work I'd done with Nicky was yet another important influence, which I've probably not said enough about. I particularly recall one session I had with her not too long before my recovery arrived. I think I had collapsed in tears and could not speak about anything much. My exhaustion was very apparent and all Nicky could do, I think, was to simply be with me, respectfully as always. Towards the end, she suggested that I could try saying to myself 'I am willing'. That was all. I asked her what I was willing for. She said it didn't matter, anything at all, or nothing at all. I shrugged, said OK, and we left it at that.

As usual, I then proceeded to forget Nicky's instructions for maybe a week or so. Then, one morning, I recalled her request to repeat 'I am willing' to myself. I pondered this again, wondering what I might be willing for. First I felt that I was being asked to say to myself that I was willing to live. But this felt like a lie, and I couldn't do it. Then I thought of some other things that I might be 'willing', such as maybe willing not to die, at least, or perhaps willing to persist with therapy. All sorts of things came to mind but none of them felt right and I was struggling with this 'I am willing' request. Because of my huge respect for Nicky, and trusting her intuitions, even when they made little sense to me, I just sat with this 'I am willing' thought for a while, without trying to make any sense of it.

The next time I saw Nicky I told her that I'd had trouble with this 'I am willing' request of hers. I told her that the best I'd been able to come up with was to say to myself that 'I am willing to be willing … to be willing … '. She guffawed with laughter and said 'Excellent!' It didn't seem quite so 'excellent' to me but her delight was spontaneous and obviously genuine. She seemed almost thrilled that I'd come up with this. I had to laugh too, though I didn't know why.

Where this fits into the overall picture during these critical few months leading up to my recovery is very hard to say, impossible really. But it somehow seems significant - along with abandoning the medications and the doctors and the surprise at finding myself drug-free, plus the personal exhaustion and the apparent exhaustion of all possible options, as well as the feeling of not being allowed to die. I was not aware at the time of all these influences working together, and still, today, it is impossible to tease out which might have been more important than others. But they all seem significant for what was about to happen.

My willingness became a willingness to surrender - though I didn't have this language for it at the time. But I did have a sense of what I was surrendering to. This I had through the teachings and the wisdom of Ramana and Gangaji. Their message was an invitation into silence. Silence, they said, again and again and again, is where to look for the answer to the 'Who am I?' question. Silence is where the true Self can be found. And this silence was the silence of a truly quiet mind, if only for a second. A silence where there are no stories of the mind about the self. A silence that called for a stop to all stories, all mental notions, of who or what I am (or might be). A silence without any shape or form. A silence that was a huge, bottomless emptiness of absolutely nothing - no thing - at all.

It's possible that I may have glimpsed this void in the past. Possibly in meditation I had felt it and took it to be just a state of mind. Possibly this was the 'black hole' of meaningless emptiness that terrorised me, making it impossible to live with myself. It can be a fine line sometimes, I reckon, between 'death-terror' and spiritual insight. In many ways this Emptiness is a very scary place to contemplate. Surrendering to it is to dive into the Great Unknown, because it is to dive into the unknowable. The mind cannot go there. It is the 'space' in which mind arises. The 'space' before and after any thought or feeling. To dwell in this 'space' as your true Self is to surrender to the possibility that your life really is as utterly meaningless as you fear. It is to surrender to and into oblivion. It is to let go of the mind as the source of your being and dare to be willing to taste this oblivion as all that you are, ever have been, or ever will be. It is to let go of all illusions of the mind as in control. It is to risk going completely stark, raving mad. It is a willingness to be annihilated.

I doubt that I could ever muster this willingness to surrender out of deliberate choice. It is just too scary. In fact, I was prepared to kill my physical body rather than dive into this Emptiness that was (and is) 'me'. But circumstances conspired, it seems, to bring me to this point of surrender, and my 'wave' came. If I'd had any other option at all, I think I would have taken it. Or if I wasn't so completely exhausted after my four years of struggle with myself, then I might have fought it. And especially, if I hadn't had the reassuring guidance of Ramana and Gangaji, I might have pulled out of this 'wave' or, indeed, ridden it clumsily into the rocks that everyone feared might be waiting for me. But there was simply nothing else I could do, nowhere else to go. That great, empty, blackhole of meaningless nothingness was calling me. And I had nowhere else to go.

But the willingness to die is so very different from wanting to die. And surrender is very different from giving up. Giving up had led me to heroin and suicide attempts. Surrendering to the silence at the core of my being, the very essence of who I am, has led me to a peace that I had never before experienced and was previously unimaginable. Within this silence all other aspects of the self arise. My body arises in this silence. My thoughts and feelings - that is, my mind - arise in this silence. This nameless silence - not my mind or any story of the mind - is the truth of who I am and where I found the peace I had been yearning for all my life and the freedom finally, at last, to just be me.

*   *   *   *   *

I tentatively called the commentary of the previous chapter the 'theory' of self-enquiry. In this chapter, which we might (even more tentatively) call the 'method' of self-enquiry, we ask *how* to embrace the silence that self-enquiry leads us to.

Spiritual self-enquiry is an invitation into the profound, unknowable silence that we find at almost the very end of our journey of self-enquiry. And silence, when we meet it, is an invitation to surrender. Surrender is a beautiful and very special word for me these days, but it also sounds rather glib and not very helpful, as it still begs the question of what surrender is and how we do it. When we are ready and the time comes, surrender is effortless. But the path to this moment is often not easy.

Before saying more about surrender, it is worth looking at some of the spiritual teachings and practices for what they can offer in this enquiry – and also what they cannot offer. I find the four schools of yoga, described in the previous chapter, quite a useful taxonomy for exploring the major types of spiritual practice. Raja yoga is the school or path of meditation with systematic practices for quietening the mind that include physical postures and special breathing techniques. Bhakti yoga is the path of faith, devotion and worship with the ultimate goal of union with God (or perhaps with your guru or Higher Power, or simply with Nature). Karma yoga is the path of altruistic, selfless service, of charity and compassion, which dissolves the individual, egoistic, personal self that separates us from Spirit, God or Nature. And gyan yoga is the path of enquiry into the nature of the self that reveals the spiritual self at the source of our being. We should note that gyan yoga includes the study of spiritual texts and scriptures, as well as the Socratic-style dialogues of Ramana's teachings.

All four schools, paths or 'methods' of spiritual practice – meditation, worship, selfless service and enquiry – are typically found in all spiritual teachings, including most religions. For instance, in Christianity there are the contemplative practices of prayer and meditation, the various devotional practices of worship, the strong tradition of Christian charity, compassion and selfless service, and also the study and discussion of the Bible and other religious texts. Although the boundaries between these practices are not always as clear-cut as suggested by the schools of yoga – for example, prayer can be both meditative and devotional – I still think it represents a useful taxonomy of spiritual practices.

With this in mind, another radical claim in Ramana's teaching is that none of these practices is actually necessary to discover the truth of who you are and realise the spiritual self. This was another shock for me. All the spiritual teachings I was familiar with required some form of practice. But for Ramana, all spiritual practices have only one purpose:

> the practice of breath-control, meditation on the forms of God, repetition of mantras, restriction on food, etc., are but aids for rendering the mind quiescent.

Ramana was frequently asked by spiritual seekers whether they should shave their heads, don the orange robes of the sadhu (the monks of yoga) and go into spiritual retreat in the forest. He invariably replied, 'Why create another obstacle to self-realisation?' It is not unusual for spiritual aspirants to become preoccupied with mastering the practices to the point of losing sight of their purpose. And in Zen there is the story of the master pointing to the moon, representing Spirit, but the student is totally absorbed in rapt adoration of the teacher's finger and fails to see what it is pointing to.

Spiritual self-enquiry points us to the silence that is all we are left with once the mind is quiet. All the other spiritual practices, like the Zen master pointing to the moon, can also help us towards this critical moment on the spiritual path. But once we reach this moment, all the practices become impotent as they cannot take you any further, but only point to what lies beyond. They can perhaps comfort us at this time with reassurance and encouragement, as we contemplate the silent emptiness before us. But that is all. No practice, no deliberate decision, can help us with the next step of this journey. Before us is the invitation into silence. We stand at the threshold of surrender.

It is here, in this knife-edge moment, that a paradox arises in the teachings of Ramana, as it does on all spiritual journeys. Self-realisation is utterly effortless, says Ramana, but effort is required to realise this. We are all familiar with the effort of living. This effort includes the journey we travel on the spiritual path leading up to the moment when we must finally let go of any effort. It is also the effort of whatever spiritual teachings we might study and practise. But most of all, it is the effort of the mind, as we've discussed at length, to create and sustain the idea – the idea – of an individual, separate self, based on the illusory self of the mind that is blind to the spiritual self in which mind arises. Effort is only required, Ramana would say, to create and sustain the illusion, the ignorance, of the mind. This ignorance, which is entirely of the mind, is the greatest obstacle to realising the spiritual self. And, paradoxically, effort is required to discover the effortless nature of our true self.

> Effortless and choiceless awareness is our real nature. If we can attain that state and abide in it, that is all right. But one cannot reach it without effort, the effort of deliberate meditation … That meditation can take whatever form most appeals to you. See what helps you to keep out all thoughts and adopt that for your meditation.

The 'deliberate meditation' referred to here can be any of the spiritual practices we've discussed, but these must always be with the purpose of quietening the mind – any practice that would help 'to keep out all thoughts'. This paradoxical effort to quieten the mind to realise the effortless nature of being is akin to another paradox found on the spiritual path. The Buddha taught that desire is the source of all suffering, but this leaves the spiritual seeker with the conundrum of the desire for desirelessness – and the endless cycle of suffering resumes. This desire for desirelessness is another effort of the mind, yet another form or instance of our ignorance. And it is overcoming this ignorance, Ramana explains, that requires effort and is the real purpose of spiritual practice:

> Removal of ignorance is the aim of practice, and not acquisition of Realisation

To say this another way, to 'know' or realise the self is effortless, but effort is required to overcome the obstacles to this realisation. These are the obstacles of ignorance, of the mistaken beliefs of the mind, and it is in letting go of these by quietening the mind where so much effort seems required. Ramana therefore endorses any effort, any practice, any 'meditation' that will assist with quietening of the mind. I once heard Gangaji capture the truth of this paradox, in rather more contemporary language:

> happiness cannot be found through the pursuit of happiness, but we need to pursue happiness to learn this

As a general rule of thumb, I personally like the suggestion that the best spiritual practice is the simplest one that works for you. But other than that, all paths are equal. As different paths to the moment of surrender – to the moment of invitation into silence – all are equally valid. The only meaningful distinction might be which one is the most appropriate for you, which would be determined by things like your personality, your social and cultural circumstances, and what practices are available and accessible to you. Although Ramana himself regarded spiritual self-enquiry as the most direct means to realising the self, he did not claim that it was necessarily the best path for any particular individual. Which is why he said 'meditation can take whatever form most appeals to you'.

But there is another path to this moment of surrender that is not usually called a spiritual practice, though it regularly arises as a topic in many spiritual teachings. This is the path of suffering. Suffering, or dukkha, is a central theme in the teachings of the Buddha, who recognised it as a universal part of the human condition experienced by us all. Initially motivated by his concern for the suffering of others, it became his own suffering as he endured the trials and tribulations of his own spiritual journey. Through his own intense personal suffering, along with prolonged study and deep meditation, he eventually realised the nature of suffering and the nature of the self that suffers. I'm no Buddhist scholar, but I see little difference between the central teachings of Buddhism and those of Ramana, other than the occasional confusion that can arise with some of the differences in terminology.

I don't want to glorify or romanticise suffering and call it a spiritual path or practice. Rather, I wish to acknowledge suffering as a noble challenge that can confront us with our deepest sense of self. This suffering can arise in life in many ways. We can see the crisis of the self that often arises with life-threatening illnesses, such as cancer. It is also seen among those approaching a 'healthy' death by old age. Such occasions in a life will often lead people to seek solace from religious or spiritual traditions, which seems perfectly appropriate to me. Another example is the intense suffering of grief that is felt at the death of a loved one, which can be especially intense if it is a premature death of, say, a child or spouse – or, indeed, a death by suicide. My own suicidality did indeed feel like an intense grieving, though I could never identify any loss that sufficiently explained its intensity. Elsewhere I have called this feeling an intense yearning, which today makes sense as the spiritual self that I was yearning for is the same 'lost' self that I was grieving for.

The point here is that any suffering that challenges our sense of self can take us into new psycho-spiritual territory. This may occur alongside some 'formal' spiritual or religious teachings that can hold our hand as we walk this difficult path. But suffering can, all by itself, take us into profound enquiry into the nature of the self that suffers. This in turn can take us – all by itself – to precisely the same moment that Ramana's self-enquiry and many other spiritual teachings point to. Suffering, by itself, can demand of us that we ask ourselves the critical spiritual question, 'Who am I?'

I am unable to tease out what contributed most to my particular journey along the spiritual path. I had the benefit of my years of yoga and, at the critical moment, the teachings of Ramana and the clear voice of Gangaji to comfort and guide me. These I acknowledge with much gratitude. But I also had the painful push (as opposed to the inviting 'pull' of silence, perhaps) of feeling never satisfied with who I was. I now acknowledge this suffering with gratitude also, including my suicidality, as central to my spiritual journey. It may sound bizarre to hear me appreciate my suicidal distress in this way, but I cannot imagine being where I am today without it. And I am so pleased to be where I am today. I am grateful for my suicidality as I am for all the spiritual teachings, and also the support of family and friends, all of which were significant for my particular journey. Suffering needs to be honoured and respected rather than denied and suppressed. It can be a great teacher that can lead us to spiritual treasures, but not if it is denied as unreal, false, illusory or delusional … or 'mental illness'.

As I said, I do not want to elevate suffering to the status of a spiritual practice – and I particularly do not want to suggest suicidality as one. As Ramana says, all these 'practices' can help but none is necessary. I firmly believe – or want to believe – that there has to be a better way than life-threatening suicidality, because suicidality has a particularly hazardous risk associated with it. It can kill you. Far too many stumble off this noble path and die. There has to be a better way, and there is. We can acknowledge the crisis of the self at the core of suicidality. We can respect and honour this self that is in crisis much more than we currently do. We can create spaces and possibilities, which by and large don't currently exist, where we can engage with and explore our sense of self more meaningfully. That is, we can create safe, spiritual spaces where we can embark on our spiritual journey, gently and in our own time, and receive guidance and companionship as we proceed, gently and in our own time. These spaces, and the possibilities that can arise in them, would be a much more healing environment for those of us struggling with suicidality than what is currently available. What's more, I believe that suicidality is much less likely to arise in a community that has these spaces where the spiritual self, and the struggles we might have with it, can be recognised, respected, honoured and nurtured.

Suicidality is a particularly acute crisis of the self that confronts and threatens everything we have thought we are, have been, or might be. Many spiritual journeys will take us to a similar confrontation. If the spiritual path is walked with gentleness and guidance, then hopefully the confrontation with the self will not be as life-threatening as suicidality, though a spiritual path totally free of any suffering seems unlikely to me, if not impossible. But once we meet this moment, when the self we know is no longer adequate, it matters little how we got here. At this moment we are standing at the threshold of the great mystery of what it is to be human, of what it is and what it means to exist and to be conscious of our existence. In Ramana's teachings this is the moment of invitation into the silence at the core of the self, the silent self that I have usually called the spiritual Self. In other teachings, such as Buddhism, this threshold is to hover at the edge of the mysterious abyss of emptiness, the great Emptiness of sunyata. In still other, more religious teachings, it might be called standing before God, with the invitation into silence being an invitation into God's embrace. Whatever language we might use for this critical moment matters little. Behind us lies a life story that has lost its meaning for us. Before us lies silent emptiness, the great unknowable mystery, or the arms of God. We cannot go back, but nor do we know how to proceed. This is the moment of surrender.

When this special moment of invitation into silence arises, it is worth pausing, as I think most people inevitably do. My story is just one of many testimonials that tells of the joy of stepping off the apparently solid threshold of the familiar and into the unfamiliar, unknowable emptiness of silence. But it is not an easy step to take. This step is the last and most difficult step on the spiritual path, and the most pressing moment of our question, 'How?' How do I let go of my attachment to my mental, psychological self? How do I let go of my sense of Spirit (or God) that still feels 'out there' and unattainable? Surrendering to this silence is the smallest, most infinitesimally tiny step, but it seems impossible. With the push of a meaningless life behind you and the pull of a glorious invitation before you, why does this last little step seem so impossibly difficult?

The first difficulty is that you cannot simply decide to take this step. Surrender is not some cognitive, mental decision. Once more we learn that the mind cannot help us here. Ramana used to say that the final obstacle is doubt. This doubt is the final clinging of the mind. Surrender into silence asks you to suspend everything you have ever known or believed. One of the most shocking sentences for me in all of Ramana's teachings was:

> There will come a time when one will have to forget all that one has learned.

This was perhaps the ultimate heresy of Ramana's teachings for someone like me, and probably the one I struggled with the most, with my robust intellect and years of education that I valued so much. It didn't make any sense to me, how could this be so? The spiritual path seemed to be almost entirely about learning. Learning the teachings and the practices. Learning about yourself. Learning about Spirit or God or whatever you called it. And here was this famous sage saying that we had to forget all we had learned. Not to mention how on earth you could ever possibly do this, even if you wanted to. Gangaji once said something similar, which also bothered me when I first heard it but it now makes so much sense to me:

> In order to give up hopelessness you must also give up hope.

In modern suicidology there is perhaps no greater heresy than this. Hopelessness is understood, quite correctly, as one of the primary feelings associated with suicidality. It is understandable then that cultivating hope is a major aim of suicide prevention. But what Gangaji is saying here is that we need to forget or let go of the mind and all it thinks, believes, and hopes for, if we are truly to 'know' the self. And this 'letting go' is to surrender to silence.

It is important at this point, with suicidality mentioned again, to emphasise that the surrender I'm speaking of here is not 'giving up' or 'giving in'. That is, surrender must not be confused with giving up and choosing death, with giving in to the urge to escape your pain by killing yourself, or with giving in and indulging the desire to die. Surrender is the difference between wanting to die and being willing to die. This distinction is a critical one.

Gangaji's words were critical for me in recognising and appreciating this vital distinction. She urges us neither to suppress nor indulge our thoughts, feelings or desires. Rather, she encourages us to allow them to arise – which they inevitably will anyway – but then not to act on them, or at least not to act on them immediately. In spiritual terms this is sometimes known as cultivating detachment from the mind by developing the sense of being the witness to the activity of the mind. In some ways this is similar to Cognitive Behaviour Therapy (CBT) and even more so to CBT's more recent cousin, Dialectic Behaviour Therapy (DBT). The difference, though, is that CBT and DBT use this as a step towards controlling our thoughts, whereas Gangaji is not at all concerned about this. On the contrary, she would encourage us to give up any fantasy of controlling our thoughts, another heresy in mental health and suicide prevention. Rather, she would urge us to spend time in the 'space' in which all thoughts arise. This is the 'space' of silence, the silent space within which all thoughts arise and into which they will all eventually subside. This is the silence that Ramana speaks of. This is the silence at the core of our being, the silence of the spiritual self. It is the space between indulging and suppressing, between wanting to die and being willing to die.

Another difficulty we might have in accepting the invitation to surrender into silence are the fears that can arise at this time. We might feel the fear of death, a legitimate fear, and indeed a kind of death does take place – and is required – to move beyond the world of mind. For some, an even greater terror might be the fear of madness, of completely losing your mind, another legitimate fear and, again, in a way this does happen – and is required. Another powerful fear is that if we step into this space then we might find that our lives really are as utterly meaningless as we sometimes suspect but dare not admit. And once more, in a way this sort of does happen – and is required. It can be frightening to stand on this threshold with the invitation into total mystery, and altogether understandable that we hesitate or retreat. Once again, I feel these legitimate fears need to be respected so that we spend whatever time with them that we need. Wise spiritual counsel would be valuable at these times too, but where do you find this these days?

These fears are once again entirely of the mind. The three mentioned above – the fear of death, madness, or meaninglessness – are all fears of some anticipated possible future that we can easily imagine at this time. The other main kind of fear likely to arise is the memory of some past pain, such as grief at the loss of someone or something dear to us. This can include a strong fear about letting go of all our past history, of the stories we have about who and what we are, which has links with the fear that your life has been utterly meaningless. These are all powerful fears that should not be dismissed lightly, so we should spend whatever time with them that we need. But to accept the invitation into silence it will become necessary to let go of them because they are all entirely of the mind and are in fact the mind clinging to these fearful stories as the truth of who and what we are.

I once heard Gangaji speak in satsang about these fears, when she was asked, 'Why do these demons keep coming back to haunt me?' The particular demons that were haunting the questioner were not specified, but Gangaji's response was one of the most significant that I heard in all her satsang. 'These fears keep coming back because the last time they visited they got fed'. These words came back to me again and again in the weeks that followed, and I came to see how very true they were. The demons are our fearful stories that require our fear to sustain them. Gangaji pointed out that these fearful stories, like any story, are entirely of the mind and always about either some remembered past or some anticipated future. And the power of these stories also comes entirely from the mind, which will happily feed them with more fear. These fears have no power at all though, none whatsoever, in the silence of a quiet mind. Or to say this another way, in the silence of a quiet mind these demons are found to be phantoms – fictions of the mind that cannot touch the silent core of our being.

I tested this. When my fearful stories, or demons, arose on the horizon of my mind, I took Gangaji's advice, so that rather than trying to fight, conquer or suppress them, I encouraged them and invited them in. I recall having an image one time of sitting on a fence (I felt like the medieval village idiot I'd seen in an old Monty Python sketch) as dark, familiar demons appear and start to approach. Instead of cowering in fear and trying to fend them off, which was my usual response and one that I knew was rarely very effective, I welcomed them and urged them on. I can recall saying to them, 'Come on down, you bastards, come and do your darndest'. I think a few times I even uttered this aloud, shouting at them and slapping the seat next to me, inviting them to join me (on my mad, medieval fence), urging them to come right on down next to me and take whatever it was they wanted. But this time I refused to feed them. I said to myself as I invited them in that they could come and do their worst, kill me even, but I was not going to feed them. I was not going to grant them the power of my mind and feed them the potent fears in my mind that they had come hunting for.

I found that Gangaji was absolutely correct. My fears had no power whatsoever other than the power I gave them. If I gave my attention to the silence at the core of my being at these times, even as the storm of fears raged in my mind, then it became like a movie. My demons were phantoms, fictions of my mind. And they couldn't touch the silence that was totally unmoved by this pathetic storm. What's more, I was able to see that all the fears were to do with either memories from the past or fantasies about the future. And in the immediate here and now of silence, where there is no time and no past or future, my demons were irrelevant. Again, the only power they had, or could ever have, was in the time and space of my mind. Without that, they could only rage and thrash about like furious wisps of smoke. And I had to laugh. Here I was getting beaten to death, almost literally, by these wisps of smoke.

Along with our fears, another likely cause for doubt and hesitation at the moment of silent invitation is any unfulfilled desires that might resurface, and possibly with great urgency. The invitation before us confronts us with the paradox of the desire for desirelessness, and any lingering desires of the mind are likely to arise with some force at this time. Again, Gangaji speaks eloquently and compassionately of this. She says that if there is anything else you desire more than the truth of who you are, then you should pursue that desire. Truth, she says, is very patient. If you still have the desire for that perfect lover, a bigger house, the next overseas holiday, or that promotion you've been working so hard for, then you should go for it and pursue these with the same commitment that is now being asked of you at this moment of truth. Because if any desires call to you more loudly than the desire to know the truth of who you really are, then truth will not compete with those desires. Truth, says Gangaji, is very silent, and very patient. And if satisfying these other desires gives you what you are looking for, well, that's fantastic. Mission accomplished. But if they fail to satisfy, or if the desire wanes, then waiting there for you, patiently in silence, is the truth of your spiritual Self, ready to welcome and embrace you.

This is another way, and I think a particularly eloquent way for western minds, of restating Ramana's apparent paradox that effort is required to discover the effortless truth of the spiritual self. It also tells me that we should not have too great a sense of urgency about striving for spiritual fulfilment. These desires that are so hard to suppress are valid and worth pursuing while they continue to be important for us.

It is certainly well worth pausing before accepting the invitation into silence. And besides, pause we must, for surrender is not a decision or choice that we can control. This feeling of no real control over our future is another fear and another reason for us to hesitate. Letting go of the need to control our lives is another heresy to modern psychology where most psychotherapies work to develop a greater sense of personal control. I'm not saying this is wrong, just that it is not appropriate at this unique moment when we are invited to surrender to the silence of the spiritual self. There is a parallel here with the struggle to resist and control death. This struggle can be a noble one, but for a peaceful death, the time comes when we must let go of our efforts to control what cannot be controlled. Like death, surrender cannot be controlled any more than it can be chosen.

We can sum up all these reasons why we might pause before surrendering to silence by seeing them all as stories demanding our attention. Our belief in the supremacy of the mind and of spirit as somehow separate from who we are right now are both stories of the mind. Both hope and hopelessness are two other psychological stories. All our fears and the psychological demons that prey on our minds are more stories, entirely of the mind's creation. Likewise our desires, dreams and fantasies, including the desire to be in control. Indeed there are many who believe that the self – or our sense of self – consists solely and entirely of all these stories we tell ourselves about who and what we are. These stories include the various theories of the self, whether they're psychological, biological, or 'postmodern' theories about the social construction of our sense of self. These latter theories of the self are particularly interesting as they often talk of 'self narratives' or the 'self as narrative', which I think is mostly quite correct and the most useful way for understanding the self of the mind. We are the stories we tell ourselves about who or what we think we are.

Except that these stories fall short in the end because they are all just stories. The rich narrative approach to understanding the psychological (mental) self, which embraces the full social and historical contexts of our stories, is certainly more sophisticated than the limited 'scientific' approach of most of mainstream psychology. And much more sophisticated than the mindless pseudo-science of modern psychiatry that reduces us all to biochemical robots. But even the rich, sophisticated and revealing narrative approach to exploring the self is ultimately inadequate because all these stories are stories of the mind. They are all just stories. They are the noisy chatter of the mind that Ramana and Gangaji urge us to put aside – if only for the briefest of moments – in order to encounter the silence in which all these stories come and go. In the end, all these stories tell us precisely nothing about the story-teller.

For me, Gangaji spoke with brilliant clarity about the limitations of these stories, and how recognising this can help us meet the challenge of surrender. These are the words I've already quoted at the opening of this chapter:

The time will come when you will have to stop with all the stories.

These words say that to accept the invitation into silence, to meet and 'know' silence – that is, to meet and know the Self – we must at some time let go of any and all stories we might have about who or what we are. All our desires, all our fears, all our beliefs, and all thoughts and feelings, must be abandoned, if only for a moment, if the depth of silence is to be revealed in all its fullness. This includes the radical heresy of Ramana that we must also let go of any notions, any teachings, any instructions, that we might have about what is Spirit (or God or enlightenment etc). Gangaji frequently repeated the one word that summed up the message of her own teacher, Papaji, which was just 'Stop'. 'Stop the search' is perhaps the phrase most frequently associated with Papaji's teachings. For me, 'Stop with all the stories' captures the essence of Gangaji's teachings. And both these messages refer back to Ramana's central message, which is to stop or quieten the mind. Just stop. If only for the very briefest of moments, because in that moment the silent stillness at the core of your being is revealed. And in that moment of silent surrender, I found peace.

Gangaji's words also hint at another key contribution to my own surrender, but not one that I would wish on others. This was the point of sheer, utter exhaustion that I had reached in my struggle to stay alive. The silence waiting for us at the end of all our stories can be seen as the time when all our stories are exhausted and no longer have any meaning or power. Coinciding with this, for me in mid-1999, was that I was physically, mentally, emotionally and socially exhausted. My life seemed meaningless and pointless so that I felt no energy for it. There was no imaginable future that I felt any desire for, nor any past history that I longed to return to. My many attempts to find some way out of this pain had all failed, and I could see no other options. Drugs, both legal and illegal, psychotherapy and counselling of various kinds, retreat to an ashram or the beautiful Australian bush – all had failed. I was physically, mentally, emotionally and socially utterly exhausted. But I also felt that I had exhausted all my options. I had even failed in trying to kill myself. I was beaten and beat. There was nowhere to go. I had no stories left. There was nowhere else for me to go. There was only the silence at the end of all my stories.

Finally, we come to the surrender. As we pause on the threshold of silence, letting go of all the stories and the mind's need to control our destiny, something quite marvellous can happen. Quietly and softly, out of the silent stillness of emptiness, a gentle peace arises. We may pause and doubt again, which is fine. But if we sit with the unknowable without wanting or needing to know but just to be, then the peace will rise. As soon as we try to grasp and comprehend this silent, still peace it will likely subside as the mind arises again and tries to name it, label it, contain it and control it. So we pause once more. Then if we ask again, 'Who am I?', and give our full attention to the silence that is the only answer to this question – peace is there. And as the peace arises, something extraordinary occurs. The peace is not rising in the silent emptiness around you. No, it is rising within me. And as it rises, I cannot see any difference between the 'I' within which this peace is now beginning to flood and the 'out there' of the silent emptiness. I cannot discern any boundary between me and the silence, now full to overflowing with peace. I find that I have become this peace. That I am peace. And then, like some cosmic joke, because you simply have to laugh at this, you see that this peace has always been there at the very core of the silent Self. Silent, still, beautiful peace is the very essence of who I am, have ever been or ever will be. Because without this silent peace that is who I am, I simply do not exist. Peace, eternal peace, always and already here, forever.

We struggle with this, of course. Or I certainly did, as doubts continued to revisit my mind. This rising wave of silent, still, unknowable peace was the 'wave' I talked about in the 'madness' chapter. This was the wave that the psychiatrist I was seeing at the time doubted, and that I doubted too, initially. But, unlike my psychiatrist, I chose to trust it. Whenever doubts arose, I turned to the silence for answers to these doubts, and always – always – the answer was this peace. For me, after four years of suicidality, this was a quite peculiar and novel feeling. And it was almost exhilarating, except that this seems an inappropriate word for the utter stillness, the total, unmoving, unchanging silence of this peace that was really quite mundane and ever so dull. This was the 'bliss' of finally meeting myself for the very first time, but not at all orgasmic or intoxicating as the word bliss suggests. And as the doubts persisted, and each time I knocked on the door of silence – there it was! Peace. Always and forever. And it could never be otherwise, because it had never been otherwise. And my suicidality became absurd.

This was my surrender. Without any 'decision' on my part, I could no longer regard my mind as the boss of who I was. Mind came and went in this silence and could never ever control it. My relationship to my mind shifted effortlessly from a domineering master to a faithful servant. Well, maybe not so faithful, as it continued – and continues – to play its little tricks as it tries to regain control from time to time. I saw that these times invariably included suffering, which became my cue – blessed suffering – to knock on the door of silence again and remember who I was. And silence reminds me that my mind is a most wonderful and wondrous servant, but a shocking master. And I laugh. Again.

We cannot decide to surrender. We can, however, decide to be open to the possibility. This is willingness, which is now another beautiful and special word for me along with surrender. Willingness is an attitude of mind that we can cultivate, explore, engage with, and work with to put some deliberate, mental effort into creating the possibility of surrender. It is Ramana's paradox again, where we can make some useful effort towards discovering the effortless nature of simply being. It is an attitude that helps us sit with the paradox of the desire for desirelessness. Willingness for me is to be open to mystery. Willingness allows the possibility of the unimaginable. And a willingness to surrender can take us into the silence in ways that the greatest spiritual teachings, the most diligent spiritual practice, or the most rigorous intellectual arguments are simply incapable of doing.

It's now time to celebrate the peace and freedom of surrender.

7

This Is Enough

A day will dawn when you will laugh at all your past efforts. That which will be on the day you laugh is also here and now.
Ramana Maharshi

For the first few months my feet hardly touched the ground. The wave that I had initially hesitated to trust proved true. I had somehow let go of my mind as the source, centre or essence of my being and learned that I was not who I *thought* I was. And I didn't collapse into a blithering madness. Instead, I was enchanted with the easy freedom that came with this deep, inner peace. I didn't have to do anything - or, rather, anything I did, anything at all, was full of enchantment and wonder. It was, I guess, quite childlike in many ways. Life was like a brand new toy. After four years in the wilderness - which I now sometimes call the 'bewilderness' - it was now a novelty and a delight to find myself actually *wanting* to be in the world.

These few months were such a treasure. And also very important. Each day that passed reinforced my surrender, and the peace became more and more tangible, more and more constantly present. It became the ground I stood on and the air I breathed. It became the reality behind all other realities. I call it 'peace' here, but I could equally call it silence, or stillness, or Self, or Spirit, or Emptiness, or 'sunya' (yoga) or 'sunyata' (Buddhism). It was in fact the completely empty, meaningless, nothingness that I had been so terrified of in my suicidal despair. And in this peace came freedom. Delightful, enchanting freedom. And I found that this simple peace and freedom was all that I had ever yearned for.

But doubts and uncertainties still arose in my mind - that busy, dratted mind again. It still felt possible that I could 'relapse' into the all-too-recent horrors that had dominated the last few years. I recall one occasion, walking in the city, when I became aware that I was getting uptight about something, that I was tightening up inside and that it was an unpleasant feeling. When I became aware of this - and this presence of mind is a very handy skill to cultivate - I realised that my mind was racing about something. I don't recall what, but I clearly recall the feeling of a busy mind that included some anger and frustration. I then recalled Gangaji's words of 'Stop, just Stop!'. Stop with all the stories. Stop with all the noisy activity of the mind. Stop, for just a moment, and ask who or what it is within you that is experiencing this noise? Stop and greet the silent Self within you, the Self in which this mental noise arises and into which it will subside. Stop and meet yourself - your Self - *that* which you simply and effortlessly *are*, already and always.

I was now becoming familiar with pausing to meet and greet this silent, inner peace that is always there but which we usually overlook. So I stopped walking. I stopped the movement of my physical body in order to pause and observe this noise in my mind. But now I witnessed the noise from the vantage point of my recently revealed spiritual Self, the source of my being. I stopped, and, ever so gently, met and greeted my Self again in a tender embrace. And there was the peace. Boundless, timeless peace. And I laughed. I laughed at the folly of my mind. I laughed that I had engaged with this mental noise to the extent that it was hurting me. I laughed at what a dope I was. I laughed at my great good fortune to be free of this attachment to my mind. And as I laughed, I celebrated and reinforced my new-found peace and freedom one more time. And once again I learned that *this that I am* was all I needed or had ever needed.

I may have got some peculiar, sideways looks from passers-by as I stood in this busy street, chuckling away at myself. Indeed I may have appeared rather 'mad'. It didn't matter at all to me. This occasion is just one of many like it that I remember well, and they are all precious and important. The noise of the mind could rise up at any time - in the street, in a conversation, privately in bed - and it did regularly. It was clear that I had definitely not 'lost' my mind. It remained very present and as active as ever. And old habits die hard, so I also frequently engaged with the mind in ways that led to some discomfort. Typically for me this would be some anger or frustration, often tinged with impatience; but it could be sadness, disappointment, worry or some other thought or feeling. There's nothing wrong with all these different thoughts and feelings - on the contrary, they are all valid and valuable parts of the human experience. But I came to recognise when they were creating some tension or discomfort in me, which became a cue to just remember, pause, and reconnect with the silent Self.

And when I bothered to make this reconnection with my silent Self - which I now could whenever I had the presence of mind to do so - I learned that this inner peace was *always* there. Whenever I 'knocked on the door' of the Self, there was this staggering, delightful peace. Always. And I was coming to recognise the truth of Ramana's and Gangaji's teaching that this peace is always there, because it is the deepest truth of who I am, of who we all are. This peace cannot *not* be there because it is the Self without which you simply don't exist. But it's a good idea to 'practise' knocking on the door and checking regularly, especially if you are a sceptical, doubting person like me.

The next thing I learned from this 'spiritual practice' was that I had a choice whether to continue to engage with this mental noise. As the witness, the detached observer of my mind, I could weigh up what was going on and make a decision (yes, with my mind) about whether I wanted to play with it or not. This 'play' could easily make me laugh as I did on that city street that day. I still regularly giggle at this 'lila' - this play of *apparent* reality - that the mind engages in so energetically. But mostly I laugh at the madness I had indulged for so many years, that this mental activity was so important. This is not to say that it is unimportant. I regularly choose to continue with these thoughts or feelings precisely because I do judge them to be important. But they were no longer central to my sense of being, my sense of self. The mind was no longer the master. My sense of self was no longer tied to my mind, my mental world. My mind was now just one aspect of my Self, in a similar way that my body is also just another aspect of my selfhood.

And I learned that the mind is a shocking master but a most wonderful servant. The mind can torment you. And there is no greater torment than the false belief that I am my thoughts, that I am who I *think* I am. Letting go of this false belief was, in fact, the surrender that set me free. In letting go of the mind as the boss, the Self that is the source of the mind is revealed. And that Self, when you dive into it, is boundless, not confined to the mental limitations of time and space. It is the Self that is always here, right now, and cannot be otherwise. Whether awake, dreaming or in deep dreamless sleep, this Self is present. The mind, which is only the presence of thoughts and feelings within our consciousness, is not required for the Self to exist. But without the Self, without consciousness, there is no mind because you simply do not exist.

I also learned that surrender is not a one-off event. Doubts continued - and continue - to arise regularly in my busy, sceptical mind. This, in turn, feeds my need to regularly test and make sense of this new sense of Self. Doubt reminds me to knock on the door of my innermost Self and maintain intimate contact with the boundless peace and freedom within me. Doubt reminds me to surrender to this peace - regularly. And the persistence of doubt requires a constant letting go of the mind, a constant willingness to surrender, a constant willingness to be me, nothing more and nothing less.

In some ways this can be seen as my primary spiritual practice these days. Sure, I meditate - irregularly, haphazardly and not very adeptly. And sure, I do some yoga, even more irregularly. And from time to time I still read spiritual texts of varying kinds. I also try to care for body, mind and soul as best I can - often pretty clumsily. But at the heart of my well-being today is the simple need to honour the spiritual Self, as best I can, and just *be me*. Not to strive to *become* me, because I can never truly be me if I am always striving to become some other version of me. Nor do I strive to be a *better* me, for there can be no 'better' me than to be fully *this that I am*, right now.

To some people this can sound like an indulgence to the ego, but nothing could be further from the truth. This spiritual Self is not the ego, which is best understood as the 'individual self', or perhaps the 'separate self'. This 'egoic self' is the self that is of the mind, the psychological or mental self. It is the self that sees itself as distinct and separate from other selves. It is the self that fears death, but which must always die, the self of desires and aversions, the self of suffering. It is also the self that contemplates suicide. I do not deny the reality and legitimacy of this egoic, mental sense of self; far from it, for it is very much a part of our day-to-day human experience. But I have learned, through self-enquiry, surrender and the constant testing of all doubts, that this individual, mental self arises from and within a deeper spiritual Self. This Self, which is not of the mental world of time and space and other thoughts, is radically different from the egoic, mental self, which, among other things, contemplates and chooses suicide. On the contrary, it is the still, silent Self of bottomless peace that set me free of my suicidal despair.

I have come to trust this Self enormously, even with the persistent doubts. It is now my trusted guide as well as my constant companion and comfort. When problems arise where I am uncertain about what decision or action to take, I turn to this Self for guidance. The process is very simple. I ask whether taking this or that path would serve to honour the Self, and if it feels like it will, then I will follow that guidance. If it doesn't, then I won't. It's not always as black and white as that so I'll sometimes have to look for other clues to help make my best guess. But always the test is whether I am being true to the Self - true to myself. But guess what, I get it wrong - frequently. I still make lousy choices and silly mistakes all too often. But with the Self as my navigator, things seem to be working out mostly just fine so far. Better than fine really.

Indeed, it has been quite 'blissful'. Bliss is a lovely word and not bad for how I felt when I stopped wanting to die. Except that for me it is a word that is often heard in spiritual circles alongside that misleading word 'enlightenment'. I also find it rather misleading for how I felt at this time because it suggests some sort of ecstatic 'high', like better than the best ever sex, or better than the best ever drug (though I'm perhaps revealing my own biases here). The 'bliss' that I felt upon my recovery was really very mundane and dull. Sure, there was the thrill of the release from my suicidal struggle, which, as I said, was truly a big thrill. But the Self that emerged and which set me free is really very ordinary. One could say extraordinarily ordinary. There were no blinding lights or orgasmic altered states of consciousness. It was simply consciousness revealed in all its glorious ordinariness. It was finally to meet myself fully for the first time in my life. It was to find a new 'home' in which my inner self could reside, except that this 'home' had always been there. It was wonderful and liberating and blissful. But it was also dull, mundane and very very ordinary. And *this* was and is enough.

I later heard this described as the Zen wisdom of 'before awakening, chop wood, carry water; after awakening, chop wood, carry water'. A similar idea is seen in the title to Jack Kornfield's terrific book, *After the Ecstasy, the Laundry*. All the mundane, day-to-day activities are still there. I still wake up in the morning and shower, toilet and feed myself. I still have chores to do that I'd often rather not have to do - karma yoga reminds me, though, of the value of these chores. And I still have my disappointments and sorrows and still, all too frequently, I can get frustrated and angry. In the first few months each and every one of these was its own delight - the whole universe visible in a grain of sand. But it didn't take too long for it to actually get rather boring. I found I was occasionally feeling restless and the constant 'blissful' enchantment was not quite so constant.

It was around this time that I started crying. I can't even say why, but I just found that I had a need to cry, usually first thing in the morning. I've never been much good at crying, neither doing it very often nor very well. My mood at this time was to just let whatever needed to happen happen. So I cried. The first one or two times it was a bit scary, not only because I didn't know why I was crying, but also because I didn't know how to do it, how to 'be with' these tears. I had one crying session when I sobbed really hard and felt the fear (again) of just how much sadness I held within me. I feared that if I didn't hold back then these tears might overwhelm me and become a flood that would never stop. But this time I dared to trust the moment and didn't hold back and the tears did eventually stop. I then proceeded to get on with that day. The next morning I cried again, and the next, and the next. Sometimes it was just a brief sob with barely a tear. Other times it surged out of me and I had to grab a towel. I just let it happen and after a while I came to appreciate it and almost look forward to it after waking up. Thankfully, I was living very alone at the time so I could 'indulge' these tears however it suited me. I let them flow. And thankfully I was also not working - I could never have permitted these tears to flow if I had to get to work on time.

I was still seeing Nicky occasionally during this early period after my recovery. I also sought out yet another counsellor, as I still felt there were 'issues' that needed to be addressed, even if I was now free of my suicidality. I found a doctor, a GP who practised his own variety of counselling therapy. He turned out to be terrific but after a month or so we agreed that whatever had changed for me, it had occurred before we'd first met. This was wonderful. Not only this man's humility and enthusiasm for my recovery, but also another confirmation that by then my recovery was emerging as robust and enduring. We joked about what the previous four years might have been like if I had met him at the start of the saga. We'll never know. There was one magic moment when we went to make our next appointment. Christmas was coming up and both he and I were planning some time out of town so our usual schedule didn't fit. As we looked into January 2000, he asked if I felt I really needed another appointment. I wondered and said to him that if I didn't make one then it would be the first time in years that I didn't have some sort of 'therapy' appointment scheduled. His immediate response was, 'So let's not make one then'. A joyous moment, a jolly good laugh, and further confirmation of my freedom.

But back to Nicky. I told Nicky about my crying which she was of course very reassuring about. She then suggested something that I found surprising. She suggested that when I cry, to cry not only for myself but for all who are suffering. I didn't really get what she was on about with this but I trusted her and said OK. As usual, I immediately forgot about her instructions for a week or so. But then one morning, as I started my now familiar crying, I recalled her suggestion. And the quiet start to that morning's tears immediately went out of control. I gasped for breath at the enormity of the sadness that rushed out of me. It was scary and for the first time I reached for the brakes and held back my tears. It was too much, much too much. I couldn't do it. I regained a little composure and wondered whether to try again. I couldn't, it was too much. So I figured out a compromise. I decided to cry just for all those who were contemplating suicide at this very moment. This was big enough but it felt possibly more manageable. These invisible, anonymous people contemplating suicide as I cried were my soulmates, my kindred spirits. I somehow felt I could cry for them. So I cried and cried, a long and beautifully sad cry. This sadness too was now another jewel in my beingness.

Eventually this morning routine of crying stopped when I went on an interstate visit. And although I still occasionally cry, partly for my many anonymous suicidal soulmates who are still suffering, it is not with the regularity or intensity of that period. I'm still not altogether sure of the significance of it and don't really need to know. But I think that perhaps I released through these tears, some (if not all) of the sadness I had carried around for so long. I think that perhaps I also learned that my sadness was not all mine, or at least not entirely *for* me. I feel little sadness for myself these days but a great sadness is still within me for all who are suffering, and especially for all who are struggling with suicidality.

It was also around this time that another moment of extraordinary grace occurred. I would occasionally drop in for a coffee and a chat with some of my old computer buddies at the university where I used to teach. A few of these old buddies knew of my struggles and had been wonderful, stalwart friends during some of the most difficult times. This time I decided to see if Elaine was still working there, who was not one of my old computer buddies but I had attended some of her workshops on teaching and learning during my early days as a lecturer. These were terrific workshops that helped me appreciate more fully the new profession of teaching that I was moving into at the time. I'd always liked Elaine, enjoying her wit and humour as well as her academic and professional talents, so I thought it would be nice to see her again after all these years. I called and made an appointment for a perfectly innocent coffee with her.

As we walked to the café she asked me what I had been doing these last five years? 'Trying to kill myself', I replied, 'What about you?'. 'Having a bit of a battle with cancer', she said. It was an extraordinary moment. In some ways we were both quite philosophical initially about each other's matter of fact answer. She was concerned, of course, to hear of my troubles, but not at all freaked out by it. And my reaction to her news was similar. The coffee break lasted nearly two hours. And we found that her efforts to live and my efforts to die had much in common.

These weekly coffee meetings went on for some time but we never seemed to find the end of this conversation. It was several months before either of us began to realise that maybe something more than a good conversation was happening between us. And several months more before this surfaced as what we now nostalgically call our unacknowledged 'courtship'. Slowly, slowly - oh, so slowly - a beautiful intimacy developed so that today we are partners in life and love. And still no sign of this conversation that we started back in late 1999 ever ending.

It seems almost ironic that this happened. I had spent a fair bit of my adult life single, which was often a source of considerable discontent for me. But now, for maybe the first time in my adult life, I was totally content to be single, unattached and not seeking intimate relationship. The joy of shedding my suicidality and the completely satisfying peace of just being me, of being *this that I am*, was a fullness that needed no 'other' to make it more full. This is not to say that I had opted for the single, celibate life like some sort of monk or swami. As Joan Armatrading once sang, I was not in love but was open to persuasion. But I did not feel the *need* for it, nor was I actively seeking it, as I had done during most of the periods of my adult life when I was single. This was very clear to me and also to Elaine by the time our conversation, in hindsight, turned out to be a 'courtship'. Elaine too was not seeking a lover. Apart from the long and still unresolved separation from her husband, the trauma of the breast cancer had left her more or less accepting that love and intimacy with a man was in her past not her future. It's hard to know who was more surprised when we found ourselves falling in love.

This was quite important as it has given a great strength to our love and life together. I suspect that some people might think that my recovery is really due to meeting Elaine. These people might also worry that if it didn't work out with me and Elaine, then I might collapse into suicidality again, given that relationship failure had been the trigger for me in the past. This would be a terrible burden for Elaine if she thought this, and for me too. Fortunately, we are both very clear about this and know that my recovery was well in place before we met for that fateful coffee break. She sees, knows and understands where the real strength of my recovery lies. And it is no slight on her or our precious intimacy to say that my stability today does not depend on her love.

Elaine knows and understands this not only because she 'sees' me very clearly. She knows it because she recognises my surrender to the silent Self as equivalent to her own surrender, to her God, that was the key to her recovery from cancer. It's not for me to tell Elaine's story here, other than to say that each of us recognised in the other this special moment of grace that we both called surrender. This mutual recognition as fellow soul survivors was further confirmation of my new sense of self that I have described here as my spiritual Self (Elaine uses different language).

In the years since, this has now been confirmed again and again. My curiosity to make sense of my story became a PhD that in turn has led to this book. During and since the PhD, I have become part of the global movement for the rights of people who experience psychosocial distress - sometimes called madness, other times mental health 'issues', but please don't call it mental illness. This in turn has brought me into the global disability movement with its slogan 'Nothing About Us Without Us', a political slogan that is a first-person statement equivalent to what this book calls for - suicide prevention needs to hear from those who know suicide 'from the inside'.

This work continues. But every step of the way, from living with Elaine to the PhD through to the global disability rights campaign, my spiritual Self has been the navigator. And again and again, it is confirmed that the most important thing for me is to be true to myself - to honour the spiritual Self that is my guide. This is not just to guide the work that I do these days. It is very much deeper than that.

I do not regard myself as 'cured' of my tendency to suicidal despair. The dark days are not forgotten and I feel no sense of guarantee that they will never return. It would be a folly to pretend otherwise. Paying attention to the spiritual need to honour the Self not only set me free from those dark days, it is also the most important thing that I must do to ensure that they do not return. Living with Elaine, the PhD and the disability rights work I do these days are all expressions of myself that honour the Self. They are all, therefore, part of what I do these days to keep myself alive and well, guided always by the spiritual Self that set me free and keeps me free.

In yoga there is the term *seva*, which is a bit like *karma yoga*. It is usually translated as service, or selfless service, or to give service, sometimes as to give service to God. For me, seva is to serve the spiritual Self as my most fundamental spiritual need and obligation. It is to give expression to that Self as best I can, such as I have tried to do through this book. It is to recognise the Self, *this that I am*, as the source of my being. *This that I am*, revealed in silence, is what I now serve and honour to the best of my ability.

This is the peace and freedom at the core of my being. *This* is my continuing journey of recovery from suicidality. *This* is the work that I do today. *This* is my daily spiritual practice that fills every moment and guides all that I do. *This* is everything and nothing, all meaning and all meaninglessness, all hope and all hopelessness. And *this* is enough.

*   *   *   *   *

The title to this chapter – *This* Is Enough – comes from Gangaji during one of her satsang, or spiritual dialogues. It might seem totally inadequate and unsatisfactory to describe the jewel that is discovered through spiritual self-enquiry with nothing more than an italicised *this*. But self-enquiry also reveals the inadequacy of any other word or thoughts we might search for to describe the spiritual Self. At the end of our enquiry we are left with no words, no thoughts, to describe what we discover.

This reminds me again of Gangaji's words from the last chapter, that the time will come when you will have to stop with all the stories. In the last chapter these words pointed to the silent Self that is the source of all our stories. But there is also another valuable message to be found in these words – that in order to find the source of our stories, they must be told. This is very much more than the simple narratives told in this book. The day-to-day living of our lives is a story that is constantly unfolding, giving expression to our lived experience of who we are. These stories are not always told in words or other narrative forms such as art, dance, music and theatre. They are told through our conversations, our body language, our relationships, our sorrows and our joys, our struggles and our victories. These stories must be told. They cannot *not* be told.

In the telling of these stories – in the living of a life – a time may come, as Gangaji says, when these stories lose their meaning, lose their power, and it is time to stop and meet the story-teller. Gangaji calls such a time in a person's life, should it arise, a blessed moment when you are being called 'home' into the silent embrace of your innermost Self. For me this moment arose through my suicidal crisis of the self. Today I treasure and honour this crisis as precisely the blessed moment that Gangaji speaks of. I do not, however, advocate suicidality as a spiritual practice. I believe we can do better than that. There are other, less dangerous ways of approaching the spiritual Self. Other stories are possible.

The stories we live are more than just our individual personal stories. They include the collective, cultural stories that are the context in which our personal stories unfold. The current story of suicide in modern Australia is an intensely negative and harmful one. Driven by fear and prejudice, it is a moralistic story that judges the suicidal as mad, bad or broken. If I listened to this story I would be deeply ashamed of my suicidal history. Although I'm not particularly proud of it, I refuse to be ashamed of it. I refuse to be shamed partly because that would deny the validity of not only my suicidal struggle but also of my recovery through spiritual self-enquiry. But most importantly of all, I reject the current story of suicide in Australia, and refuse to be shamed by it, because I cannot think of anything that poses a greater risk to me of those dark days returning.

There are other elements to the current thinking about suicide – our collective, cultural stories about suicide – that are equally toxic. These too must be told if we are to move beyond them. In particular, we need to move beyond the medical fundamentalism that labels the noble suicidal crisis a 'mental illness'. We need more options for the suicidal than just which anti-depressant they should take. Rather than these and other shallow stories around suicide, we need a collective story that is capable of accommodating the full depth and complexity of the suicidal crisis of the self. And for this, we need to hear from those who know suicidality 'from the inside' – more stories that must be told.

In this book I have used two distinct voices, the narratives and the commentaries, to distinguish between the personal and the collective stories. As we now approach the end of all the stories in this book, these two voices begin to converge. The narrative of this chapter celebrates my liberation from four years of suicidal struggle. It also hints at the life I live today since this peace and freedom arrived. This brings us to the work that I now do, and in particular my research into suicide. This is the voice of the commentaries where I analyse and challenge much of the current thinking about suicide. So in some ways the commentaries are at least part of the narrative of the life I live today.

I have no autobiographical urge to bore you with my life story since my recovery. But by way of concluding this book there's perhaps one or two stories that can be told. Perhaps the main one is that, by rather peculiar circumstances, I found myself enrolling in a PhD to do some in-depth study into suicide. Having read my story this far, you will not be surprised to hear that my motivation for this was to try and bring some spiritual ideas into our current thinking about suicide. Initially. I was not at all optimistic that this would be possible in a university setting where spirituality is usually seen as too unscientific for serious academic study. It was my great good fortune, however, to find a path through these prejudices with the help of some terrific staff at the university.

I also don't want to bore you with the full academic argument of my thesis, which the interested can find elsewhere. But a couple of key moments of that story are relevant to the story here. I expected to find spirituality largely absent from the academic thinking about suicide, but I was not prepared for the almost equal absence of what I now call the first-person voice of suicidality. This is the voice of the lived experience of those who know suicidality from the inside, which you will recognise as a central theme throughout this book.

I was taken aback by just how rarely the first-person voice appeared in the literature of suicidology, but as my research proceeded it became apparent why this is so. It is typically excluded because it is seen as unscientific – anecdotal, subjective, unreliable, etc. – but this could be challenged without too much difficulty. Many other academic disciplines these days have moved beyond these narrow prejudices about what constitutes valid knowledge. There had to be something more to suicidology's exclusion of the first-person voice than just these tired old prejudices.

I'll return to this shortly, but first I need to mention some other, non-academic work I was doing around this time. I was becoming increasingly involved in what is called the mental health 'consumer' community. For a while I identified as a 'consumer' but no longer do so as I regard it as just another oppressive label of the mental health industry. If need be, I will these days identify as a psychiatric survivor, but the point here is that alongside my suicide research I was getting involved in mental health politics. And guess what, the first-person (consumer, survivor) voice was largely absent here also. Not as much as it was missing from suicidology, but the marginalisation or 'tokenism' of the first-person voice was – and still is – one of the hot issues in mental health politics.

There are three main reasons why the first-person voice is largely excluded from suicidology and mental health in general. The first, as mentioned above, are the prejudices against first-person knowledge as valid scientific data or evidence. These prejudices are most severely found in medicine and psychiatry, but they are also common in psychology and the social sciences. The second reason is rather obvious, though you're not allowed to actually say it. Our voices do not have credibility because, obviously, virtually by definition, we are mad! This rather obscene prejudice is particularly severe in suicidology but is common throughout mental health – like the elephant in the room that must not be mentioned. The third reason, which is based on the previous two, and is the most obscene prejudice of all, is our mental health laws.

It was my political work, rather than my research, that led me to our mental health laws and other human rights issues. There are many other serious issues in mental health, such as the need for non-medical alternatives and the lack of funding for services that we mostly hear about. But the critical issue is society's discrimination against people labelled as 'mentally ill'. This is usually called stigma, but we need to call it by its correct name, discrimination. And the primary source of this discrimination is mental health laws that take away our citizenship on the basis of a psychiatric diagnosis. This is the ultimate denial of the first-person voice, because these laws make us non-persons.

The consequence of all these prejudices is very much more severe than just the poor understanding of suicide that we find in suicidology. I have come to the view that our mental health laws actually contribute to the suicide toll. To be locked up and have drugs forced on you is an assault on your person – some call it torture, others describe it as rape, but at the very least it must be seen as an assault. I can think of few things that are less helpful, and indeed harmful, for someone who is already feeling suicidal. This seems obvious to me, perhaps because I see suicide as a crisis of the self rather than the consequence of some notional mental illness. But whether you agree with me or not, it is extraordinary that we do not even ask if our mental health laws help or hinder suicide prevention. These laws are simply assumed to be necessary based on status quo assumptions which in turn are based on fear, ignorance and prejudice. I am not aware of any study that looks at either the efficacy or the safety of these laws for suicide prevention. If they were regarded as a medical intervention then there is no doubt that they would not be permitted with so little evidence to justify them.

These days, as I find myself increasingly involved in the human rights arena, I occasionally have to remind myself – and my colleagues – that the original motivation for my research was to try and bring some spiritual ideas into our thinking about suicide. But then I have to remind myself (and my colleagues) that there is a direct link between suicide and spiritual ways of knowing, the first-person voice, and human rights. Through my research it became apparent that we would never get spirituality onto the suicide prevention agenda while the first-person voice continued to be banished from suicidology. And through my political work I learned that the first-person voice would continue to be banished while society maintained its discrimination against suicide and madness – discrimination that is expressed most fully in the mental health laws that we have.

So I occasionally feel some sadness that I have had to join the sometimes grim struggle for mental health human rights when I'd really rather be talking about how spiritual wisdom can help us understand suicide better. But this conversation is all but impossible in a society that regards the suicidal person as less than human. We cannot speak of our spirit unless we can first reclaim our voice. The fight for the human rights of suicidal people must be fought, to allow the first-person voice, and then spiritual ideas, into our current thinking about suicide.

Despite the many frustrations, and not much income, most of the time the disability rights work that I now do is extraordinarily satisfying and rewarding. It feels very much like precisely what I need to be doing at this time in my life. In particular, this work allows me to live my life truly, which is the most important thing I must do to ensure that suicidality does not return.

This final chapter is therefore not just a celebration of discovering the Self that set me free from persistent suicidality. It is also a celebration of the Self that guides me as I live my life today. I described this in the narrative as the need to be true to myself – to honour the spiritual Self that is my guide and navigator. I also said that I still make plenty of clumsy mistakes. Although *this* is enough, and I seek nothing more than *this that I am*, I am no tranquil saint basking in eternal spiritual bliss. After I found myself actually wanting to live in the world again, all the usual stories resumed very quickly. I still get upset and angry. I still make other people upset and angry. I still make errors of judgement and I still doubt myself, frequently. But I no longer doubt the Self that is the source of who I am. Nor do I doubt that my well-being today depends on being true to myself – to the indescribable, ineffable *this that I am*.

Once again, an italicised *this* seems inadequate, even though we have seen how it is inevitable that any words or thoughts will always be inadequate. But I have recently come across some words that are as good as I've heard for this obligation to be true to yourself. They come from Parker Palmer, a distinguished American scholar who writes beautifully about the sacred in his field of teaching and learning. He says the biggest decision that any person can make in their life is to decide to live 'divided no more'.

'All around us', says Palmer, 'dividedness is presented as the sensible, even responsible, way to live'. We are all familiar with the divided life as the mismatch we all feel at times between our inner and outer worlds, but sometimes 'there are extremes of dividedness that become intolerable'. At these times we might also realise that this dividedness is not entirely due to external forces but 'comes also from the fact that I collaborate with these forces, giving assent to the very thing that is crushing my spirit'.

Palmer calls the decision to live divided no more the 'Rosa Parks decision' in honour of the woman who decided, 'one hot Alabama day in 1955, that she finally would sit at the front of the bus'. Although Rosa Parks' decision on this day was also a political statement that sparked the modern civil rights movement in the US, Palmer also sees in it her realisation that 'there is no punishment worse than conspiring in a denial of one's own integrity'. Rosa Parks chose to live divided no more and no longer participate in her own oppression.

Living the divided life is an apt description for the origins of my suicidal crisis of the self. It is also an apt description of my participation in my own oppression, trapped as I was in the divided self of the mind. It is also apt for the cultural divisions we find between the medical, psychological and spiritual ways of thinking about suicide. And what I discovered when I surrendered to the silent embrace of my innermost self is also described well as an end to living a divided life. Finally, my well-being today rests on the decision – indeed the obligation – to live divided no more.

And *this* is enough.

Om shanti ...

FURTHER READING

One of the aims of this book is to encourage a conversation about suicide in plain language that everyone can be a part of. For this reason, I've included very few references, footnotes or citations etc, which can often get in the way of a book's 'readability'. Some readers, however, will be disappointed by this and want to see the reference material that I've drawn upon in writing *Thinking About Suicide*. I'll mention just a few key references below, but the curious or studious reader can find complete and comprehensive references and other information at the book's companion website:

www.thinkingaboutsuicide.org

Thinking About Suicide was the primary volume of my two volume PhD. The second volume, known as the 'exegesis', contains the formal academic argument of my thesis, including references to its extensive bibliography, and can be found at the website. You will also find information about my work since completing *Thinking About Suicide*, which I will try to keep up to date. For anyone wishing to contact me, this can be done through the website, and perhaps there will be a forum or blog where visitors can raise and comment on any topics of interest that might arise. I welcome any feedback on the book or the website and hope that it will help to encourage the community conversation on suicide that *Thinking About Suicide* calls for.

Suicidology
Professor Edwin S. Shneidman
Professor Edwin S. Shneidman was a pioneer of suicidology back in the 1950s and the first President of the American Association of Suicidology (AAS) whose annual award for contributions to the field carries his name. As a psychologist he laments, as I do, the current trend in recent decades towards the increasing medicalisation of suicidality. Professor Shneidman died in 2009, aged 91.

The Suicidal Mind is perhaps his classic work, and *Comprehending Suicide* is included here because it is Professor Shneidman's own thoughtful selections of classics from the literature of suicidology. But please read anything and everything that you can get your hands on by this giant of the field who, unlike many of his modern contemporaries, never turned his back on the actual suicidal person.

Shneidman, ES (1996) *The Suicidal Mind*. Oxford: Oxford University Press.
— (2002) *Comprehending Suicide: Landmarks in twentieth century suicidology*. Washington, DC: American Psychological Association.

The Aeschi Group

(http://www.aeschiconference.unibe.ch/)

The Aeschi Group are about a dozen eminent and innovative suicidologists who meet every two years in the Swiss town of Aeschi. Mostly academic clinicians, their focus is on therapeutic responses to suicidal distress, but from a perspective that challenges the prevailing mainstream ideas and practice in suicidology. In particular, they continue the legacy of Professor Shneidman in putting what suicidal people say about their suicidal feelings at the centre of their practice. The best source for the group is their website shown above, which outlines their approach and includes references to published works of group members and other useful references. For me, the Aeschi Group represents the only innovative, critical and creative voice in modern suicidology and the hope for the future of the discipline. Strongly recommended.

Suicide Attempt Survivors

In stark contrast to the boom industry of books on so-called depression, there's remarkably few first-person accounts of suicide attempt survivors. *The Savage God* is something of a classic that needs to be mentioned, although it's more about Alvarez' close friend, Sylvia Plath, than his own suicidality. The books by Susan Rose Blauner and Terry Wise are both important and significant first-person accounts of surviving suicidality – pity about the title of Blauner's book, though. Kay Redfield Jamison is quite famous as a psychiatrist who has written magnificently about her own bipolar diagnosis and clearly knows suicidality 'from the inside' in *Night Falls Fast*. Styron's small and gentle book is beautifully written, though he tends to talk more about his depression than his suicidal feelings. But I'm particularly fond of John Miller's selection of passages by great writers in *On Suicide*.

Alvarez, A (1971) *The Savage God: A study of suicide*. Harmondsworth: Penguin.

Blauner, SR (2002) *How I Stayed Alive When My Brain Was Trying to Kill Me: One person's guide to suicide prevention*. New York: HarperCollins.

Jamison, KR (1999) *Night Falls Fast: Understanding suicide*. New York: Alfred A. Knopf.

Miller, J (ed) (1992) *On Suicide: Great writers on the ultimate question*. San Fransisco: Chronicle Books.

Styron, W (1992) *Darkness Visible*. London: Picador.

Wise, TL (2003) *Waking Up: Climbing through the darkness*. Los Angeles: Pathfinder

Critiques of Modern Psychiatry

It's becoming hard to keep up with the increasing literature on the bankruptcy of modern psychiatry. I just mention three of my favourites here but look out also for Richard Bentall's latest book, *Doctoring the Mind: Why Psychiatric Treatments Fail*. Bob Whitaker (*Mad in America* and *Anatomy of an Epidemic*) and John Read (*Models of Madness*) are two other authors worth reading.

Bentall, RP (2003) *Madness Explained: Psychosis and human nature.* Harmondsworth: Penguin.

After soundly debunking the Kraepelian assumptions of the *DSM*, the highly credentialled clinical psychologist, Richard Bentall, calls upon comprehensive and compelling research to show that madness is not a medical mental illness of the brain but a natural, normal and indeed very human psychological response to very human life events. He shows that the boundary between sanity and madness is very much in the eye of the beholder and that the greatest threat to the well-being of the mad is often the fear of madness.

Lehmann, P & Stastny, P (eds) (2007) *Alternatives Beyond Psychiatry.* Berlin: Peter Lehmann Publishing.

Sixty-one authors from all around the world, many of them psychiatric survivors, discuss humane alternatives to the madness of modern psychiatry. It is published by Peter Lehmann, one of its co-editors, who also edited and published *Coming off Psychiatric Drugs*, another important reference. His website – www.peter-lehmann-publishing.com – is also recommended for its extensive bibliography of other related books and articles (including some by me).

Hornstein, G (2009) *Agnes's Jacket.* New York: Rodale Books.

Gail Hornstein is an academic psychologist who has had a lifelong passion for the first-person voice of madness. *Agnes's Jacket* is a superbly crafted narrative of Hornstein's years of research that assembles a great many voices of those who know madness 'from the inside' into a powerful message of humanity and hope, but also another damning indictment of modern psychiatry.

The (Postmodern) Self

Contemporary thinking about the self is central to my thinking about suicide and was therefore central to my PhD research. As this can be a rather dry and academic topic for some readers, I've not spent much time on this in *Thinking About Suicide* other than in the Interlude. I'll also leave it for interested readers to visit the website for more detailed references, except to mention here just a few of the key influences – and recommended authors – on my thinking about the self.

Ken Wilber

Ken Wilber has been a particularly strong influence with his Integral Model, which I regard as the most comprehensive, accessible and holistic model for our sense of self (selfhood) – indeed these days I use the Integral Model as my definition of holistic. It's hard to convey the extraordinary breadth and depth of Wilber's prolific writings, which some people find rather too colourful for serious scholarship, though I love it. I was first drawn to Wilber's work because spiritual ways of knowing are central to his approach, rather than tacked on to the periphery as it is in most academic discussion of spirituality, which rarely works.

Although the 800+ pages of *Sex, Ecology and Spirituality* is Wilber's 'magnum opus' where his Integral Model is spelt out in detail, I would recommend either *The Marriage of Sense and Soul*, or my personal favourite, *The Eye of Spirit*, for an initial taste of his ideas. If your interest is specifically in psychology (or mental health) then *Integral Psychology* is succinct but comprehensive. For his personal reflections on spirituality then *One Taste* is a book you can dip into at random, or spend some time with the delightful *Simple Feeling of Being*, an edited collection of his spiritual contemplations from his other books. Much spiritual wisdom will also be found in the moving story of his wife Treya's battle with breast cancer in *Grace and Grit*.

Wilber, K (1991) *Grace and Grit: Spirituality and Healing in the Life and Death of Treya Killam Wilber*. Boston: Newleaf.
— (1998) *The Marriage of Sense and Soul*. New York: Random House.
— (2000) *Integral Psychology: Consciousness, spirit, psychology, therapy*. Boston: Shambhala.
— (2000) *One Taste: Daily reflections on integral spirituality*. Boston: Shambala.
— (2000) *Sex, Ecology, Spirituality: The spirit of evolution*. Boston: Shambala.
— (2004) *The Simple Feeling of Being: Embracing your true nature*. Boston: Shambala.

Wilber's Integral Model is the framework used in my own research to propose a more comprehensive approach to suicide and suicidality, which I call Integral Suicidology. There is now a growing community developing the Integral Model in a wide range of fields so perhaps the best place to start is to visit the website of the Integral Institute – www.integralinstitute.org – or for a complete list of his book, and also some downloadable papers etc, visit his webpage at his publishers – wilber.shambhala.com

Dan Zahavi

Dan Zahavi's work only appeared within my intellectual horizons towards the end of my PhD research. Since then I've became a great fan – indeed if I was 20-30 years younger I'd be knocking on his door begging him for some post-doctoral position at his Center for Subjectivity Research in Copenhagen. For me, Zahavi is at the forefront of rediscovering the true genius of Edmund Husserl, the father of phenomenology whose profound insights into the nature of consciousness have been largely lost in the fog of postmodern twaddle of the latter half of the 20th century. His book *The Phenomenological Mind*, co-authored with Shaun Gallagher, is especially good and much recommended.

Zahavi, D & Gallagher, S (2008) *The Phenomenological Mind*. New York: Routledge

Francisco Varela and colleagues
Francisco J. Varela is a neuroscientist with a particular interest in the cognitive aspects of the mind and consciousness. With his colleagues, he has pioneered the idea of bringing spiritual wisdom into the study of the mind, in particular using Buddhist mindfulness training to reach more deeply into the subjective, first-person data of cognitive experience. His 1993 book with Evan Thompson and Eleanor Rosch, *The Embodied Mind*, is a landmark and still 'essential reading' in the field. Sadly, Varela died just prior to the publication of *On Becoming Aware*, which was a major reference for my own research.

Varela, FJ, Thompson, E & Rosch, E (1993) *The Embodied Mind: Cognitive science and human experience.* Cambridge, MA: MIT Press

Depraz, N, Varela, FJ & Vermersch, P (eds) (2002) *On Becoming Aware: A pragmatics of Experiencing.* Amsterdam/Philadelphia, PA: John Benjamins

David Chalmers
I need to mention David Chalmers, not because he's Australian but because his papers on consciousness are both brilliant scholarship and beautiful writing. His idea of experiential knowledge as the 'hard problem' of consciousness is still the acid test for research in the field, as is the idea that consciousness cannot be explained by the reductive methods of traditional science but has to be understood as an irreducible property of the universe, like gravity. Mind boggling stuff. Except Chalmers himself clings to the *belief* that consciousness is an attribute of the mind, whereas I – and spiritual sages such as Ramana – would say the opposite, that mind is an attribute of consciousness. The debate continues, at least in some quarters, thankfully.

Spiritual Teachings of Ramana Maharshi and Gangaji
Ramana's teachings are now more widely available in the west, though still not commonplace. The tiny booklet *Nan Yar* remains my personal treasure of his printed teachings. It can now be downloaded from the website below under the title 'Who Am I?' David Godman's compilation of Ramana's teachings are also a treasure.

Godman, D (ed) (1985) *Be as You Are: The teachings of Sri Ramana Maharshi.* Harmondsworth: Penguin/Arkana.

Website: http://www.ramana-maharshi.org/

Gangaji's main means of sharing the teachings of her lineage is via satsang, including video and audio recordings of the public satsang she has held, which you can download or purchase at the following website:

Website: http://www.gangaji.org/

ACKNOWLEDGEMENTS

During my 'four years of madness' I often distanced myself from – even shunned – many of the people I cared for and who cared for me. But a few managed to penetrate my self-imposed isolation and be with me during this time. I'd particularly like to thank Susan Humphrey, Janty Taylor, Steve Hayes, Daryl D'Souza, Margie Joyce, Susie Russell, Greg Hall and Lisa Intemann for their loving support during those times when I was not very lovable.

There are others who also sustained me during these difficult years but must remain nameless, some because I never knew or have forgotten their names, while some must remain anonymous to respect their privacy. These are the people I met in the drug rehabs, at AA and NA meetings, on the psychiatric wards and on the street. It also includes many of the psychiatric survivors that I've met since those dark days. This book is motivated by and dedicated to all those who struggle with life, whether it be suicide, addictions, trauma or any other challenge to our sense of self. I acknowledge you all, with love and hope and confidence.

There are some psychiatric survivors who I am able to acknowledge by name. These are just a few of the growing chorus of survivors who are leading the global campaign for a radical re-thinking of how we understand and respond to psychosocial distress. Peter Lehmann, David Oaks, Tina Minkowitz, Mary Nettle, Jasna Russo, Bhargavi Davar, Gabor Gombos, Sylvia Caras, Mary O'Hagan, Chris Hansen, Iris Hoelling and Moosa Salie – I thank you and all our comrades, for your courage, your solidarity, and for all that you have taught me. Nothing About Us Without Us!

There are other teachers, in the more formal sense of the word, who I must acknowledge for without their support and guidance this book would probably never have been realised. In particular, Professor Ron Adams bravely dared to be the principal supervisor of my rather unorthodox PhD research project. It is hard to imagine completing this work without his deft touch and fearless good humour. And my second supervisor, Mark Stephenson, complemented Ron's guidance brilliantly with his spiritual, but scholarly, insights into the questions I was investigating. My warm thanks also go to David Mithen, Cath Roper and Susan Pepper for their thoughtful and constructive criticisms of the final draft of the book prior to it being submitted for examination as part of my PhD.

I offer special thanks to Josephine Williams (not her real name) who, as a fellow suicide attempt survivor, inspires and encourages me that we can and must think and talk about suicide differently.

There are three other people I must also thank for the timely completion of my PhD: its three examiners, Professor Valerie Walkerdine, Professor David Jobes and Dr Jacques Boulet, each of whom made a valuable, critical assessment of my thesis. I thank Valerie once more for the quite brilliant foreword (please read it again) that she has generously written for this published version of the book. David's important work as a suicidologist with the Aeschi Group is acknowledged elsewhere in the book, but I would like to add here my personal thanks for the support he has given me as a dissenting voice within suicidology, and also for granting permission to quote from his examiner's report on the back cover. And special thanks also to Jacques who came to the rescue at the last minute after one of my original examiners had to withdraw.

Many thanks also to Maggie Taylor-Sanders and Heather Allan, and everyone at PCCS Books who bravely dared to publish this unlikely book. PCCS Books have repeatedly shown their commitment to the first-person voice of madness and I feel privileged to join their list of very fine books and authors.

Finally, I must acknowledge my immediate family who endured so much during my struggles but were always there for me. My mother Sonya would have delighted in my graduation but she sadly, though peacefully, died in 2004. But she did live to see me finally win my freedom, which was a far greater joy for her than any graduation ceremony. Her beloved partner of 56 years, my father Bob, was at my graduation in 2006 but will miss the launch of this book, passing away in 2008, age 89. Bob was the most enthusiastic supporter of my work with his usual flair for daring to ask the hard questions with a wit and humour that never wavered. Twin brother Mike and sister Barb, who make brief appearances in this book, were often in the front line of my madness when it was burning hot – frightening, bewildering, frustrating, sometimes infuriating. But never did their love waver, though at times it was the 'tough love' often required at these times, perhaps the toughest love of all to give. Sisters Megan and Sally were not quite as close to it being so far away geographically, but their love and support were always near. And Megan's own journey of recovery continues to be a joy and inspiration for us all. It's doubtful if I could have done a project such as this book, and the accompanying PhD, if anyone in my family, especially my mum or dad, had asked me not to, which many families might. But I have only ever received support and encouragement from this extraordinary family.

Before finishing, I must now also acknowledge the new 'family' that has appeared in my life since I stopped wanting to kill myself. It is impossible to describe Elaine's contribution to my work as my first reader, my keenest critic, and my closest confidante on this literary journey and now, it seems, in life. Her kids Leo and Helen, now with their partners Victoria and Simon, have warmly and generously welcomed this stranger into their mother's life, contributing their own intelligent, youthful wisdom to my work. I'm especially pleased that Helen allowed me to use her extraordinary painting as the cover for the book, and thanks also to Simon for taking the great photo of it that made this possible. And now, Helen and Simon have given us young Mallee, another teacher for me, this time teaching me how to be a grandad without ever having been a dad.

Needless to say, the responsibility for any arguments, errors, points of view or opinions expressed in this book rests entirely with me.

I now finish and at the same time start all over again by once more bowing low and humbly acknowledging, with silent, nameless reverence, the hundred or so people in Australia who will try to kill themselves today, six or seven of whom will succeed ...

David Webb, Melbourne, 2010

.

FLESH WOUNDS?

NEW WAYS OF
UNDERSTANDING
SELF-INJURY

KAY INCKLE

ISBN 978 1 906254 29 2

RRP £18.00

Flesh Wounds? features fictionalised real-life stories drawn from a two-year research project. Kay Inckle challenges the stigmatising view of self-injury as something 'mad' or 'bad', highlighting the importance of understanding each individual's complexity. She illustrates the experiences that might lead to self-injury, and which responses are helpful and which are not. The book acts as a resource for people who hurt themselves and for those who live and work with them. *Flesh Wounds?* points towards the need for a holistic and person-centred understanding of self-injury, focusing on harm reduction rather than prevention.

Dr Kay Inckle lectures in qualitative research methods and ethics in the School of Social Work and Social Policy in Trinity College Dublin, where she has also established a certificate course in understanding and responding to self-injury from a harm-reduction ethos. Her work with self-injury spans a range of experience including as a social care practitioner, as a PhD and post-doctoral researcher, as a trainer to service providers, as a lecturer, academic and activist. Her work is informed by her pursuit of theory, research and practice which manifest alternative, non-exploitative ways of knowing and being.

PCCS Books   www.pccs-books.co.uk
sales@pccs-books.co.uk   +44 (0)1989 763900

PCCS Books

independent publishing for
independent thinkers